MS.CHUCK'S
PATCHWORK

Foreword

When I was touring Japan with a quilt exhibition, I had the opportunity of meeting and talking with many quilters in each city. I had always liked big, flat quilts but by talking with those quilters, I began to realize what their desire was. I knew many of them had beautiful quilts at home but being in the exhibition hall, I could not see them. However, I saw many carrying patchwork quilted bags. I knew from that time that I wanted to write a book only about bags! Fortunately, the publisher had the same idea and my students agreed to cooperate. In a matter of a very short time, I was able to finish this book.

Quick and easy, yet fashionable and convenient : these were the concepts I had in mind. All of the projects can be finished in half a day or up till two weeks. I hope my readers will enjoy this book and I hope to meet someone someday on the streets carrying one of these bags.

Chuck Nohara

Copyright© 1989 ONDORISHA PUBLISHERS, LTD. All rights reserved.
Published by ONDORISHA PUBLISHERS, LTD., 11-11 Nishigoken-cho, Shinjuku-ku, Tokyo 162
Sole Overseas Distributor: Japan Publications Trading Co., Ltd.
P. O. Box 5030 Tokyo International, Tokyo, Japan.
Distributed in United States by Kodansha America, INC.
114 Fifth Avenue, New York, NY 10011, U.S.A.
in British Isles & European Continent by Premier Book Marketing Ltd.,
1 Gower Street, London WC1E 6HA, England
in Australia by Bookwise International
54 Crittenden Road, Findon, South Australia 5023, Australia

10 9 8 7 6 5

ISBN 0-87040-820-8

Printed and bound in Japan

Sawtooth Tote Bag and Ribbon Bag

Using the crisp angles of triangles, I have created a soft and delicate tote bag for special occasions. I have used a white background but by experimenting with other colors, you can get different effects.
The little Ribbon Bag is perfect as a gift which any receiver would love!

Instructions on page 2.

(Materials)
Background fabric, backing fabric, batting
......80cm × 40cm (31½" × 15¾") each
Assorted scraps of print fabric

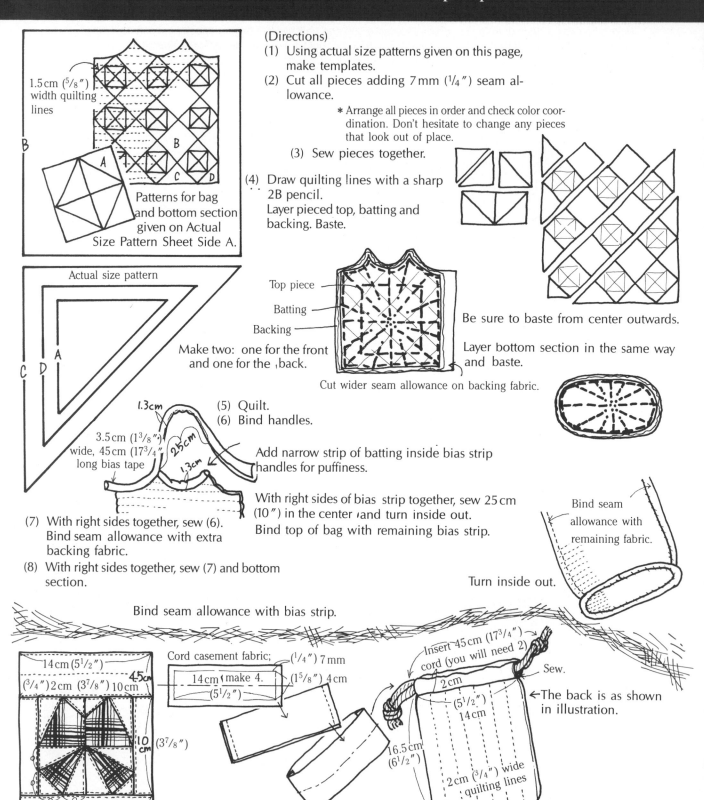

1.5cm (⅝") width quilting lines

B

A
B
C D

Patterns for bag and bottom section given on Actual Size Pattern Sheet Side A.

Actual size pattern

C D A

(Directions)
(1) Using actual size patterns given on this page, make templates.
(2) Cut all pieces adding 7 mm (¼") seam allowance.
  * Arrange all pieces in order and check color coordination. Don't hesitate to change any pieces that look out of place.
(3) Sew pieces together.
(4) Draw quilting lines with a sharp 2B pencil. Layer pieced top, batting and backing. Baste.

Top piece
Batting
Backing

Make two: one for the front and one for the back.

Cut wider seam allowance on backing fabric.

Be sure to baste from center outwards.

Layer bottom section in the same way and baste.

(5) Quilt.
(6) Bind handles.

1.3cm
3.5 cm (1⅜") wide, 45 cm (17¾") long bias tape
25cm
1.3cm

Add narrow strip of batting inside bias strip handles for puffiness.

With right sides of bias strip together, sew 25 cm (10") in the center and turn inside out.
Bind top of bag with remaining bias strip.

(7) With right sides together, sew (6). Bind seam allowance with extra backing fabric.
(8) With right sides together, sew (7) and bottom section.

Bind seam allowance with bias strip.

Bind seam allowance with remaining fabric.

Turn inside out.

14cm (5½")
(¾") 2cm (3⅞") 10cm
45cm
10 cm (3⅞")
2cm

Cord casement fabric;
(¼") 7 mm
14cm make 4.
(5½")
(1⅝") 4 cm

Insert 45 cm (17¾") cord (you will need 2)
2cm
Sew.
(5½") 14cm
16.5 cm (6½")
2cm (¾") wide quilting lines

←The back is as shown in illustration.

(Measurements for Ribbon Bag)

Strip-quilted Travel Case and Pouch.........P. 96

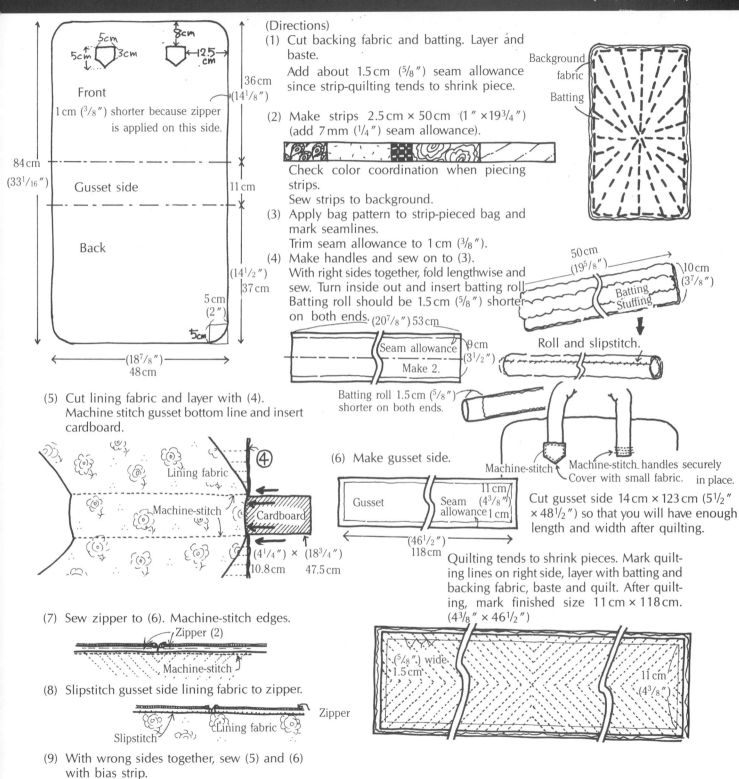

(Materials)
Backing fabric, lining fabric, batting......
150 cm × 80 cm (59″ × 31¹/₂″) each
Assorted scraps of print fabric
1 60 cm (23¹/₂″) Zipper
Polyester stuffing
Cardboard......50 cm × 50 cm (19³/₄″ × 19³/₄″)

Front
1 cm (³/₈″) shorter because zipper is applied on this side.

5cm 5cm 3cm 8cm 12.5 cm

Gusset side

Back

36 cm (14¹/₈″)
11 cm
84 cm (33¹/₁₆″)
(14¹/₂″) 37 cm
5 cm (2″)
5cm
(18⁷/₈″) 48 cm

(Directions)

(1) Cut backing fabric and batting. Layer and baste.
Add about 1.5 cm (⁵/₈″) seam allowance since strip-quilting tends to shrink piece.

(2) Make strips 2.5 cm × 50 cm (1″ × 19³/₄″) (add 7 mm (¹/₄″) seam allowance).
Check color coordination when piecing strips.
Sew strips to background.

(3) Apply bag pattern to strip-pieced bag and mark seamlines.
Trim seam allowance to 1 cm (³/₈″).

(4) Make handles and sew on to (3).
With right sides together, fold lengthwise and sew. Turn inside out and insert batting roll.
Batting roll should be 1.5 cm (⁵/₈″) shorter on both ends.

Background fabric
Batting

50 cm (19⁵/₈″)   10 cm (3⁷/₈″)
Batting Stuffing
Roll and slipstitch.

(20⁷/₈″) 53 cm
Seam allowance
Make 2.
9 cm (3¹/₂″)
Batting roll 1.5 cm (⁵/₈″) shorter on both ends.

Machine-stitch   Machine-stitch handles securely
Cover with small fabric.   in place.

(5) Cut lining fabric and layer with (4).
Machine stitch gusset bottom line and insert cardboard.

④
Lining fabric
Machine-stitch
Cardboard
(4¹/₄″) × (18³/₄″)
10.8 cm   47.5 cm

(6) Make gusset side.

Gusset   Seam allowance 1 cm
11 cm (4³/₈″)
(46¹/₂″) 118 cm

Cut gusset side 14 cm × 123 cm (5¹/₂″ × 48¹/₂″) so that you will have enough length and width after quilting.

Quilting tends to shrink pieces. Mark quilting lines on right side, layer with batting and backing fabric, baste and quilt. After quilting, mark finished size 11 cm × 118 cm. (4³/₈″ × 46¹/₂″)

(5/₈″) wide.
1.5 cm
11 cm (4³/₈″)

(7) Sew zipper to (6). Machine-stitch edges.
Zipper (2)
Machine-stitch

(8) Slipstitch gusset side lining fabric to zipper.
Zipper
Lining fabric
Slipstitch

(9) With wrong sides together, sew (5) and (6) with bias strip.
(10) Sew zipper end to bag!

Pattern for the purse is shown on the actual-size pattern for Side A. Check out the instructions for the other bags and make those, too!

3

Pyramid Bag and Purse

PYRAMID BAG

I used earthtone colors, black and off-white, to create a sophisticated bag set that can be used at formal times.

Instructions on pages 6, 7.

MS.CHUCK'S
PATCHWORK
[pách'wûrk']

A kind of fancy work in which pieces of cloth differing in color and shape are sewn together,

oftentimes to form a design,

and which is used in covering quilts,

pillows, etc.; hence,

a similarly variegated or checkered appearance or scene,

as a patchwork of fields.

Pyramid Bag and Purse

................................PP. 4, 5

(Materials)
Black fabric······80 cm × 40 cm (31¹/₂″ × 15³/₄″)
White fabric······1 m × 30 cm (39³/₈″ × 11³/₄″)
Assorted scraps of print fabric
Batting······110 cm × 40 cm (43¹/₄″ × 15³/₄″)

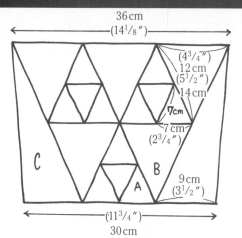

36 cm
(14¹/₈″)
(4³/₄″)
12 cm
(5¹/₂″)
14 cm
7cm
7 cm
(2³/₄″)
C
B
A
9 cm
(3¹/₂″)
(11³/₄″)
30 cm

Patterns for C and bottom section are given on Actual Size Pattern Sheet Side A.

(Directions)
(1) Make cardboard templates.
(2) Cut pieces adding 7 mm (¹/₄″) seam allowance.
Arrange pieces in order and check color coordination.
(3) Sew pieces together.

(4) Mark quilting lines with sharp 2B pencil. Layer with batting and backing fabric. Baste.

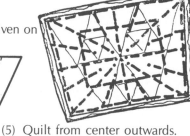

Baste from center outwards as shown in illustration.

Layer and baste bottom section.

(5) Quilt from center outwards.

Insert needle 2–3 cm (³/₄″–1¹/₄″) from starting point and take one stitch, pull knot and cut.

The knot will disappear into batting. Quilting stitches should be the same size on front and back. (About 8–9 stitches per 3 cm (1¹/₄″) is perfect!)

(1¹/₄″)   -- < actual size >
3 cm

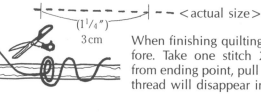

When finishing quilting, do as you did before. Take one stitch 2–3 cm (³/₄″–1¹/₄″) from ending point, pull thread and cut. The thread will disappear into batting.

B

Fold

A

Actual size pattern

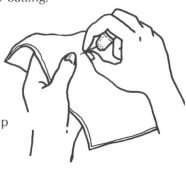

*When quilting, be careful not to bunch up the layered piece with your hand.

(4) With right sides together, sew two (5).

(7) With wrong sides together, sew (6) and bottom section with bias strip. Bias strip should be 5 cm (2″) width. Apply batting for puffiness.

(8) Sew handles.

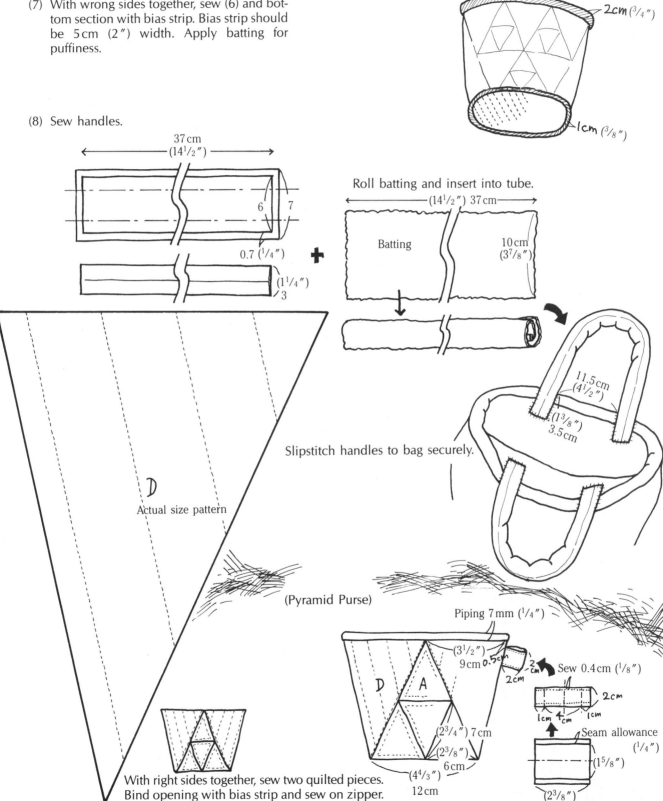

2cm (³/₄″)

1cm (³/₈″)

37 cm
(14¹/₂″)

6   7

0.7 (¹/₄″)

(1¹/₄″)
3

+

Roll batting and insert into tube.

—(14¹/₂″) 37 cm—

Batting

10 cm
(3⁷/₈″)

11.5 cm
(4¹/₂″)

(1³/₈″)
3.5 cm

Slipstitch handles to bag securely.

D
Actual size pattern

(Pyramid Purse)

Piping 7 mm (¹/₄″)

(3¹/₂″)
9 cm 0.5 cm

2cm

2cm

Sew 0.4 cm (¹/₈″)

2cm

1cm 4cm 1cm

D   A

(2³/₄″) 7 cm

(2³/₈″)
6 cm

Seam allowance
(¹/₄″)

(1⁵/₈″)

With right sides together, sew two quilted pieces.
Bind opening with bias strip and sew on zipper.

(4⁴/₃″)
12 cm

(2³/₈″)

CIRCLE BAG

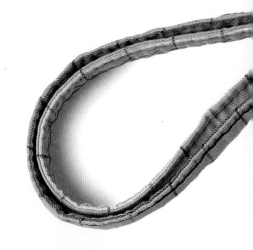

Pieced Donkey Circle Bag and Coin Purse

Baby donkey following Mother donkey? This is Jody's favorite set of bags. There is room for a lot and don't worry if it gets heavy. There are shoulder straps. Finishing the circle bags may seem difficult but if you follow the instructions carefully, they are quite easy.

Instructions on pages 10, 11.

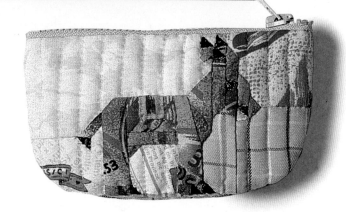

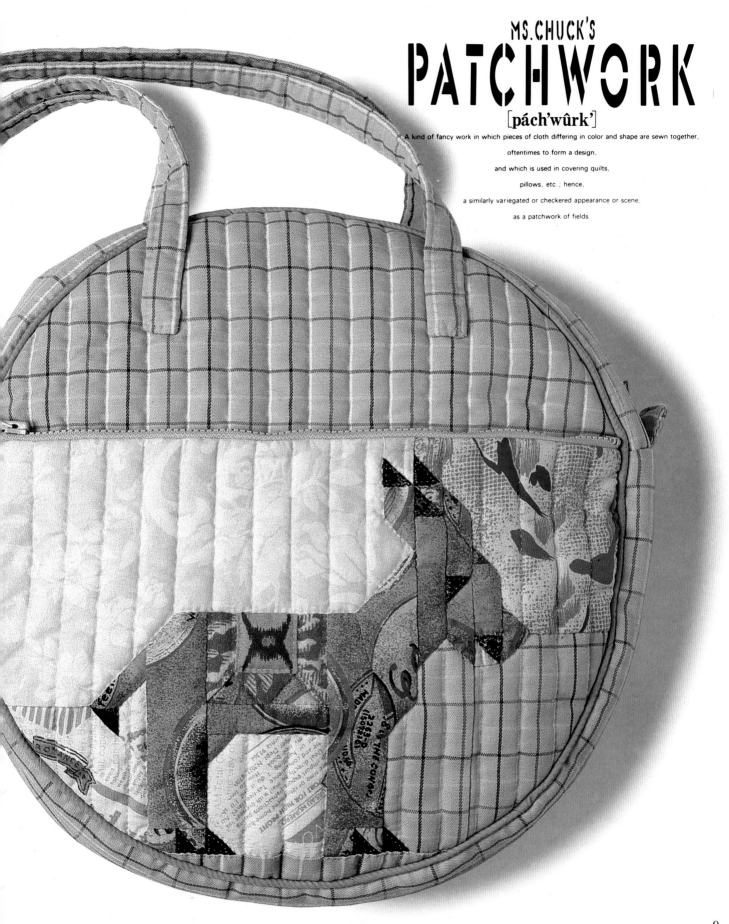

MS.CHUCK'S
PATCHWORK
[pách'wûrk']

A kind of fancy work in which pieces of cloth differing in color and shape are sewn together,

oftentimes to form a design,

and which is used in covering quilts,

pillows, etc.; hence,

a similarly variegated or checkered appearance or scene,

as a patchwork of fields.

(Materials)
Background fabric······90 cm × 70 cm
(35¹/₂″ × 27¹/₂″)
Backing fabric, batting······120 cm × 50 cm
(47¹/₄″ × 19³/₄″) each
Assorted scraps of print fabric
1 40 cm (15³/₄″) zipper

(Directions)
Patterns are given on Actual Size Pattern Sheet Side A.

(1) Make Donkey pocket.
  (a) Make cardboard templates.

  (b) Cut pieces with 7 mm (¹/₄″) seam allowance.
     Arrange pieces in order and check donkey's colors in coordination with bag.

  (c) Join pieces.

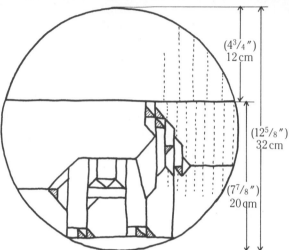

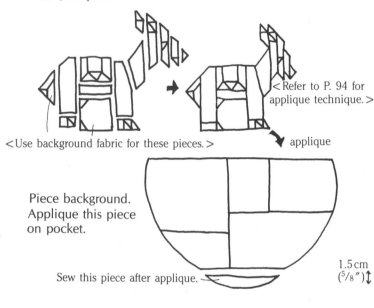

< Refer to P. 94 for applique technique. >

< Use background fabric for these pieces. >

applique

Piece background.
Applique this piece on pocket.

Sew this piece after applique.

Mark matching notches around circle bag and the same number of notches on gusset side and zipper.
The more notches, the easier it will be to join pieces.

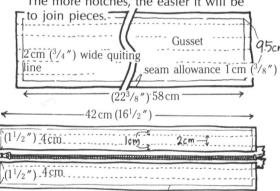

Gusset

9.5 cm

2 cm (³/₄″) wide quiting line

seam allowance 1 cm (³/₈″)

(22³/₈″) 58 cm

42 cm (16¹/₂″)

1.5 cm (⁵/₈″)

(1¹/₂″) 4 cm   1 cm   2 cm

(1¹/₂″) 4 cm

Seam allowance 1 cm (³/₈″)

(2) Layer all sections with batting and backing fabric.
    Baste.

Back side   Front side

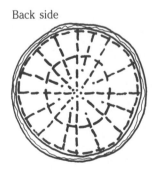

Pocket

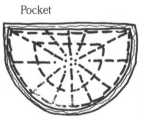

Zipper (Both side)

Gusset

(3) Quilt all sections. Apply pattern and mark finished size. Trim seam allowances to same width.

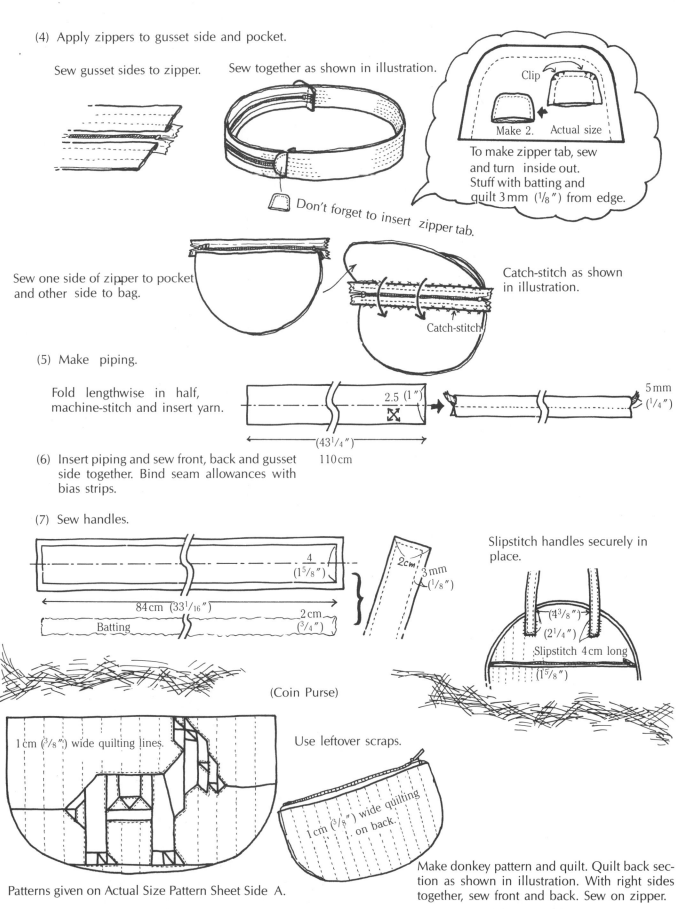

(4) Apply zippers to gusset side and pocket.

Sew gusset sides to zipper.

Sew together as shown in illustration.

Clip

Make 2.   Actual size

To make zipper tab, sew and turn inside out. Stuff with batting and quilt 3 mm (1/8″) from edge.

Don't forget to insert zipper tab.

Sew one side of zipper to pocket and other side to bag.

Catch-stitch as shown in illustration.

Catch-stitch

(5) Make piping.

Fold lengthwise in half, machine-stitch and insert yarn.

2.5 (1″)

5 mm (1/4″)

(43 1/4″)
110 cm

(6) Insert piping and sew front, back and gusset side together. Bind seam allowances with bias strips.

(7) Sew handles.

4 (1 5/8″)

2cm
3 mm (1/8″)

84 cm (33 1/16″)

2 cm (3/4″)

Batting

Slipstitch handles securely in place.

(4 3/8″)

(2 1/4″)

Slipstitch 4 cm long

(1 5/8″)

(Coin Purse)

1 cm (3/8″) wide quilting lines.

Use leftover scraps.

1 cm (3/8″) wide quilting on back.

Patterns given on Actual Size Pattern Sheet Side A.

Make donkey pattern and quilt. Quilt back section as shown in illustration. With right sides together, sew front and back. Sew on zipper.

11

Quilted White Bag and Tulip Lingerie Case

Wouldn't you like a white quilted bag with shirred handles for very special occasions? The pineapple pattern and close quilting create an attractive yet sturdy bag.
It would be so romantic to go on a trip with this sweet and delicate lingerie case. It is a three-fold case and there are two compartments inside.

Instructions on pages 14, 15.

MS.CHUCK'S
PATCHWORK
[pách'wûrk']

A kind of fancy work in which pieces of cloth differing in color and shape are sewn together,

oftentimes to form a design,

and which is used in covering quilts,

pillows, etc.; hence,

a similarly variegated or checkered appearance or scene;

as a patchwork of fields.

Quilted White Bag

....**P. 13**

(Materials)
Background fabric, batting······1 m × 60 cm
(39³/₈″ × 23¹/₂″) each
Backing fabric······1 m × 40 cm (39³/₈″ × 15³/₄″)
Assorted scraps of print fabric
Lining fabric······1 m × 50 cm (39³/₈″ × 19³/₄″)

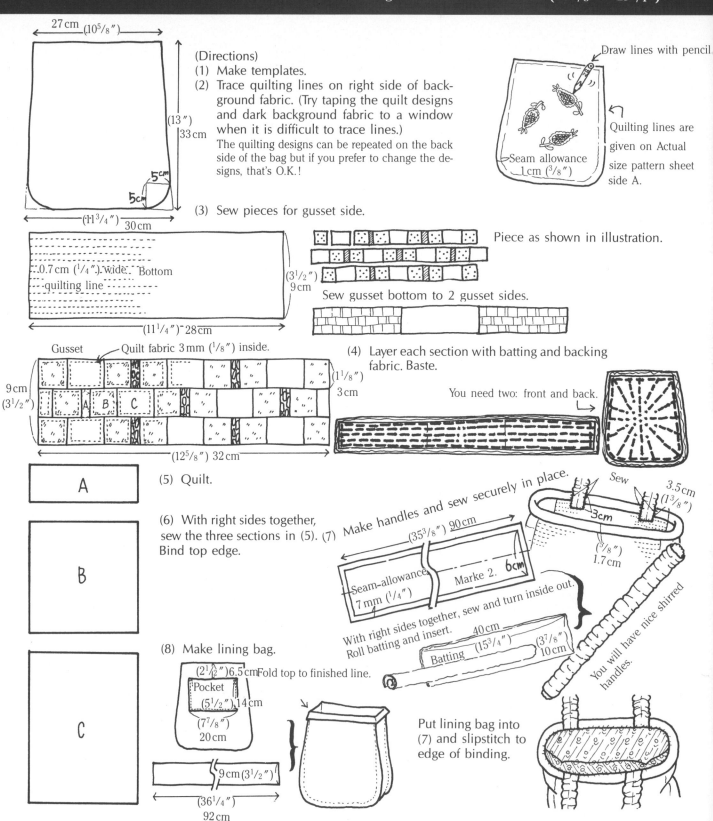

27 cm (10⁵/₈″)

(13″) 33 cm

5 cm
5 cm

(11³/₄″) 30 cm

(Directions)
(1) Make templates.
(2) Trace quilting lines on right side of background fabric. (Try taping the quilt designs and dark background fabric to a window when it is difficult to trace lines.)
The quilting designs can be repeated on the back side of the bag but if you prefer to change the designs, that's O.K.!

Draw lines with pencil

Quilting lines are given on Actual size pattern sheet side A.

Seam allowance 1 cm (³/₈″)

(3) Sew pieces for gusset side.

0.7 cm (¹/₄″) wide Bottom quilting line

(11¹/₄″) 28 cm

(3¹/₂″) 9 cm

Piece as shown in illustration.

Sew gusset bottom to 2 gusset sides.

Gusset   Quilt fabric 3 mm (¹/₈″) inside.

9 cm (3¹/₂″)

A B C

(1¹/₈″) 3 cm

(12⁵/₈″) 32 cm

(4) Layer each section with batting and backing fabric. Baste.

You need two: front and back.

A

(5) Quilt.

(6) With right sides together, sew the three sections in (5). (7) Bind top edge.

(7) Make handles and sew securely in place.

(35³/₈″) 90 cm

Sew

3.5 cm (1³/₈″)

3 cm

(⁵/₈″) 1.7 cm

Seam-allowance 7 mm (¹/₄″)

Marke 2.   6 cm

B

With right sides together, sew and turn inside out. Roll batting and insert.

40 cm
Batting (15³/₄″)   (3⁷/₈″) 10 cm

You will have nice shirred handles.

(8) Make lining bag.

C

(2¹/₂″) 6.5 cm Fold top to finished line.

Pocket
(5¹/₂″) 14 cm

(7⁷/₈″) 20 cm

9 cm (3¹/₂″)

(36¹/₄″)
92 cm

Put lining bag into (7) and slipstitch to edge of binding.

(Materials)
Background fabric, backing fabric, batting
......60cm × 40cm (23^1/$_2$″ × 15^3/$_4$″) each
Assorted scraps of print fabric
Lining fabric......80cm × 60cm (31^1/$_2$″ × 23^1/$_2$″)
Lace (5cm (2″) wide)......4m (157^1/$_2$″)
2 Ribbon (3.5cm (1^3/$_8$″) wide)......50cm (19^3/$_4$″)
Elastic (5mm (^{1}/$_4$″) wide)......70cm (27^1/$_2$″)
1 Heart-shaped button

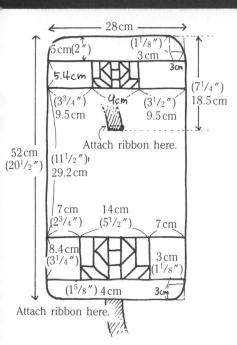

28cm

5cm(2″) (1^1/$_8$″) 3cm

5.4cm 3cm

(7^1/$_4$″) 18.5cm

(3^3/$_4$″) 9.5cm 4cm (3^1/$_2$″) 9.5cm

Attach ribbon here.

52cm (20^1/$_2$″)

(11^1/$_2$″) 29.2cm

7cm (2^3/$_4$″) 14cm (5^1/$_2$″) 7cm

8.4cm (3^1/$_4$″) 3cm (1^1/$_8$″)

(1^5/$_8$″) 4cm 3cm

Attach ribbon here.

(Directions)
(1) Make templates. Pattern is given on Actual Size Pattern Sheet Side A.
(2) Choose fabrics.
Cut tulip pieces adding 7mm (^{1}/$_4$″) seam allowance. Add 1cm (^{3}/$_8$″) seam allowance for all other pieces. Arrange pieces in order and check color coordination.

(3) Sew pieces together.
(Refer to P. 38 for piecing order of tulip)
(4) Layer (3) with batting and backing fabric.
(5) Quilt.
(6) Make inner side.

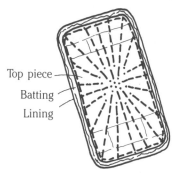

Top piece
Batting
Lining

Make casement for elastic at top edge of pocket. Insert 31cm (12^1/$_4$″) elastic and gather. Make little pleats at bottom and baste with small stitches on lining fabric.

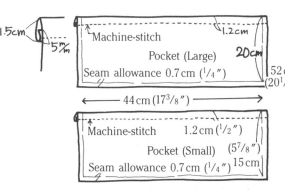

1.5cm
5㎜
Machine-stitch 1.2cm
Pocket (Large) 20cm
Seam allowance 0.7cm (^{1}/$_4$″)

← 44cm (17^3/$_8$″) →

Machine-stitch 1.2cm (^{1}/$_2$″)
Pocket (Small) (5^7/$_8$″)
Seam allowance 0.7cm (^{1}/$_4$″) 15cm

28cm (11^1/$_4$″)

Sew elastic firmly. (6^1/$_4$″) 16cm

52cm (20^1/$_2$″)

Sew here.

20cm (7^7/$_8$″)

15cm (5^7/$_8$″)

(7) Sew lace ends to make circle. Gather and place on (5) with right sides together.

5cm (2″) wide × 4m (157^1/$_2$″)

Distribute gathers evenly but allow slightly more fullness around corners.

(8) With right sides together, sew (7) and (6), be sure you have top and bottom in the correct position. (Refer to illustration for correct position)

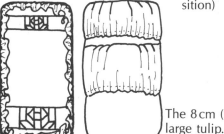

The 8cm (3^1/$_8$″) opening should be below large tulip.

Turn inside out through opening. Insert one ribbon and slipstitch opening.
Sew other ribbon to designated position.

Sew on heart-shaped button.

Japanesque Strip-quilted Bags

The overall effect changes according to the diagonal or horizontal placement of the fabric strip. You can get a variety of designs using Japanese fabric.

Instructions on pages 18, 19.

JAPANESQUE POCHETTE

MS.CHUCK'S

PATCHWORK
[pách'wûrk']

A kind of fancy work in which pieces of cloth differing in color and shape are sewn together,

oftentimes to form a design,

and which is used in covering quilts,

pillows, etc.; hence,

a similarly variegated or checkered appearance or scene;

as a patchwork of fields.

Japanesque Strip-quilted Bags......................P. 16

(Materials)
Assorted scraps of print fabric
Backing fabric, lining fabric......40cm × 30cm
(15³/₄″ × 11³/₄″)
Black fabric......30cm × 20cm (11³/₄″ × 7⁷/₈″)
Batting......40cm × 30cm, 150cm × 5cm
(15³/₄″ × 11³/₄″, 59″ × 2″)
1 20cm (7⁷/₈″) zipper

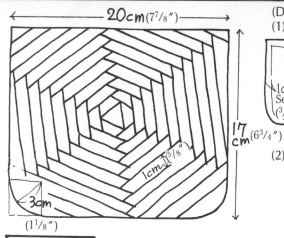

20cm(7⁷/₈″)

17cm(6³/₄″)

1cm(³/₈″)

1cm(³/₈″)

3cm
(1¹/₈″)

Center triangle
(actual size)

(Directions)

(1) Layer backing fabric and batting. Baste.

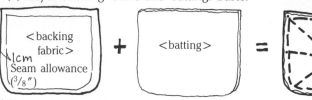

<backing fabric>
1cm
Seam allowance
(³/₈″)

<batting>

(2) Place triangle with 7mm (¹/₄″) seam allowance in center (or anywhere near center). Refer to P. 54 for strip-quilting technique. In this case, apply strips in circles.

(3) Make back section.

Lining
Batting
Top piece

Draw quilting pattern that you like.

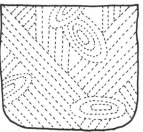

I did mine in a Japanese design which looks like swept sand in a rock garden.

(4) Cut 2 pieces of lining fabric in the same size as backing fabric. Layer with (2) and (3) and bind top edge.

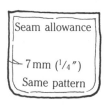

Seam allowance

7mm (¹/₄″)

Same pattern

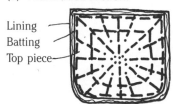

7mm(¹/₄″)

Lining fabric
(内布)

Hand-sew zipper.
Sew other side.

(5) With wrong sides together, sew (4) together with bias strips.

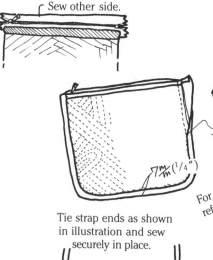

7mm(¹/₄″)

(6) Make strap.
With right sides together, sew and turn inside out.

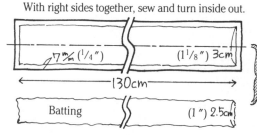

7mm(¹/₄″)   (1¹/₈″) 3cm

130cm

Batting   (1″) 2.5cm

Tie strap ends as shown in illustration and sew securely in place.

For finishing ends of strap, refer to P. 31.

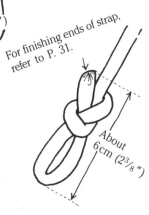

About 6cm (2³/₈″)

Japanesque Strip-quilted Bags ·········· P. 17

(Materials)
Background fabric, lining fabric······40 cm × 30 cm (15³/₄″ × 11³/₄″)
Assorted scraps of print fabric
2 Cords······65 cm (25¹/₂″)
#5 Embroidery floss

(Directions)
(1) Make templates.
(2) Choose fabrics. Cut pieces adding 7 mm (¹/₄″) seam allowance.

(3) Sew pieces together.
Use thin fusible interfacing on silks for easier piecing.
With right sides together, sew pieced front section and back section.

(4) Make lining bag.

(5) With right sides together, sew top of (3) and (4) and turn inside out at opening.

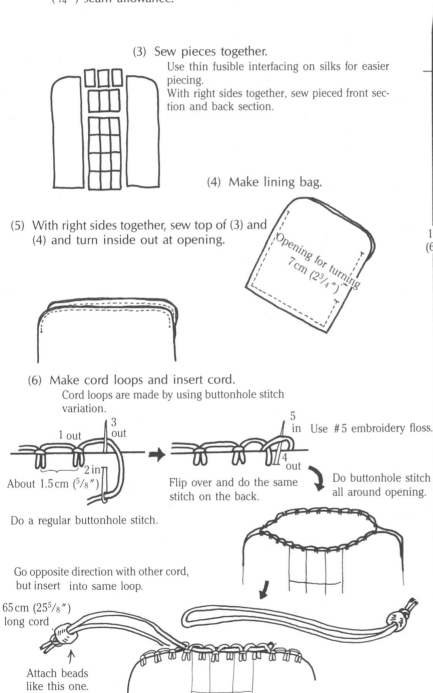

(6) Make cord loops and insert cord.
Cord loops are made by using buttonhole stitch variation.

1 out   3 out

About 1.5 cm (⁵/₈″)   2 in

Do a regular buttonhole stitch.

5 in Use #5 embroidery floss.

4 out

Flip over and do the same stitch on the back.

Do buttonhole stitch all around opening.

Go opposite direction with other cord, but insert into same loop.

65 cm (25⁵/₈″) long cord

Attach beads like this one.

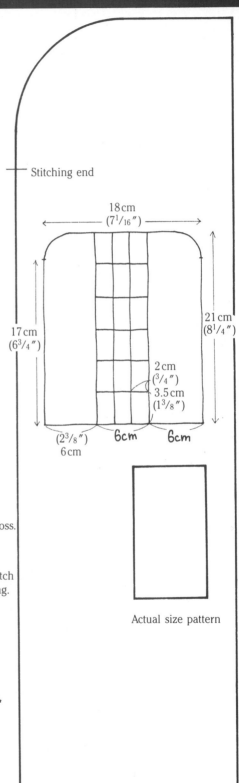

Stitching end

18 cm (7¹/₁₆″)

17 cm (6³/₄″)

21 cm (8¹/₄″)

2 cm (³/₄″)
3.5 cm (1³/₈″)

(2³/₈″) 6 cm   6 cm   6 cm

Opening for turning 7 cm (2³/₄″)

Actual size pattern

TRIANGLE

Triangle Drawstring Pouch

Though this is a simple pattern, you need to play with your fabric and choose carefully. I experimented with authentic Japanese fabrics like Oshima, Ai-zome (indigo-dyed fabric) and "Sake" (Japanese liquor) bag material. Changing the fabric or using brighter colors, you have a totally different effect.

Instructions on pages 22, 23.

MS.CHUCK'S
PATCHWORK
[pách'wûrk']

A kind of fancy work in which pieces of cloth differing in color and shape are sewn together,

oftentimes to form a design,

and which is used in covering quilts,

pillows, etc.; hence,

a similarly variegated or checkered appearance or scene;

as a patchwork of fields

Triangle Drawstring Pouch ....PP. 20, 21

(Materials)
Assorted scraps of print fabric
Backing fabric, batting……70 cm × 20 cm
(27½″ × 7⅞″)
Indigo-dyed fabric……80 cm × 30 cm
(31½″ × 11¾″)
2 65 cm (25½″) Cords

(Directions)
(1) Make cardboard templates.

(2) Keeping color coordination in mind, cut pieces adding 7 mm (¼″) seam allowance. Arrange pieces in order and check color balance.

(3) Sew pieces together.

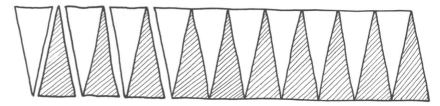

(4) With a sharp 2B pencil, draw quilting lines. Layer with batting and backing fabric. Baste.

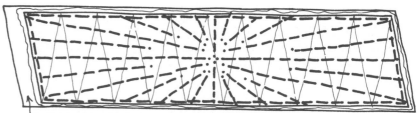

Cut backing fabric larger than pieced top. Extra backing fabric will be used to bind seam allowance.

Layer and baste bottom section in the same way.

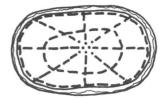

(5) Quilt.

Bind seam allowance with extra backing fabric.

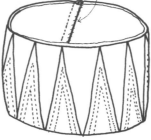

(6) Sew side seams of pieced top.

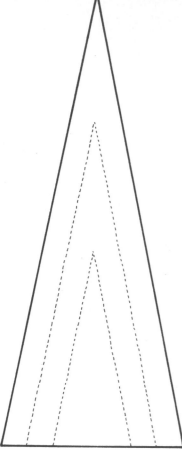

Actual size pattern

22

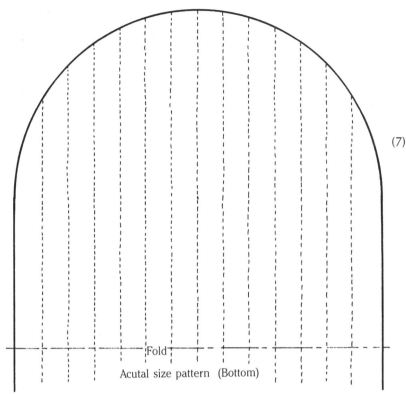

Fold

Acutal size pattern (Bottom)

(7) With wrong sides together, sew pieced top and bottom section. Bind seam allowance with bias strip.

Sew bias strip with pieced top and bottom section for a nice finish!

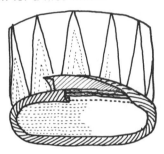

(8) Sew opening section.

10 cm (3⁷/₈″)

7 mm (¹/₄″)

Fold

4 cm (1⁵/₈″)

10 cm (3⁷/₈″)

1.5 cm (⁵/₈″)

Cord casement

⟵—— 25 cm ——⟶

11 cm (4³/₈″)   Don't sew.   11cm

Open seams and turn inside out.
Fold in half.

4 cm (1⁵/₈″)

1.5 cm (⁵/₈″)

Machine-stitch cord casement line.

With right sides together,
sew opening fabric and
pieced top.

Fold at finish line and slipstitch to backing fabric.

(9) Insert cord.   < 2 65 cm (25⁵/₈″) cords >

Attach ornament to cord ends.

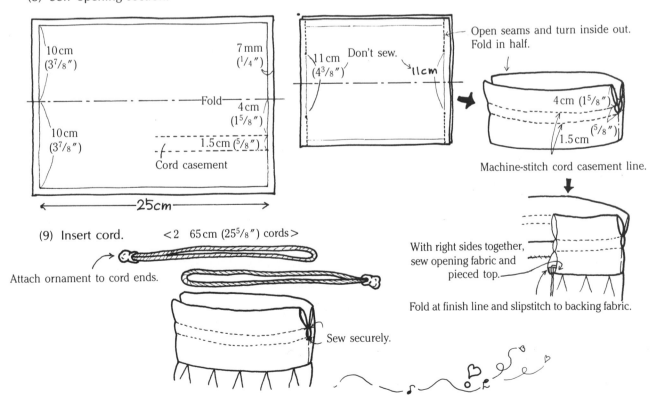

Sew securely.

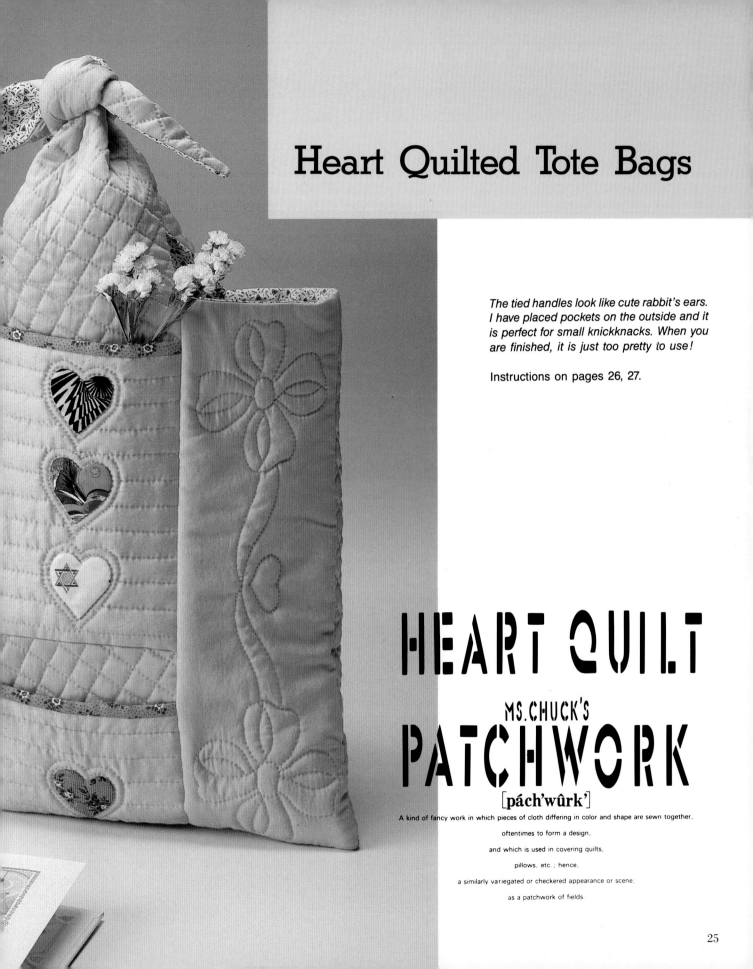

Heart Quilted Tote Bags

The tied handles look like cute rabbit's ears. I have placed pockets on the outside and it is perfect for small knickknacks. When you are finished, it is just too pretty to use!

Instructions on pages 26, 27.

HEART QUILT
MS.CHUCK'S
PATCHWORK
[pách'wûrk']

A kind of fancy work in which pieces of cloth differing in color and shape are sewn together,

oftentimes to form a design,

and which is used in covering quilts,

pillows, etc.; hence,

a similarly variegated or checkered appearance or scene,

as a patchwork of fields.

(Materials)
Background fabric, backing fabric, batting
······**80 cm × 80 cm (31 1/2″ × 31 1/2″) each**
Assorted scraps of print fabric

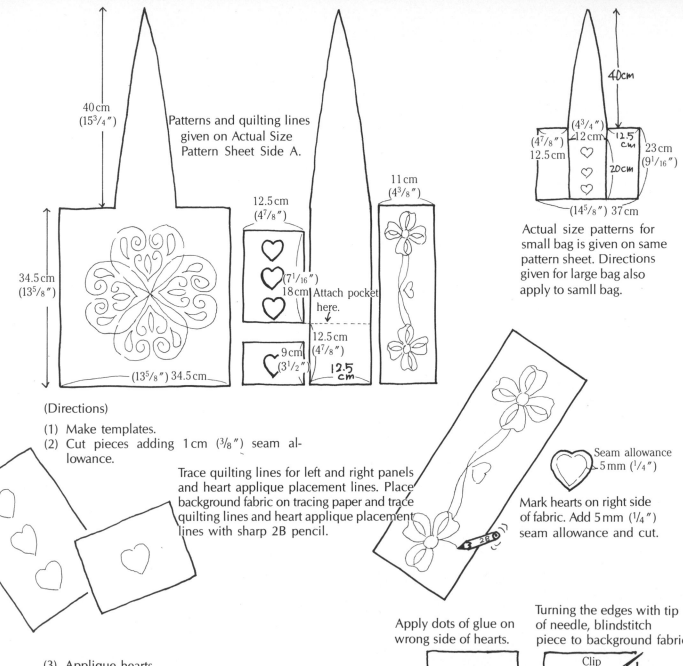

Patterns and quilting lines
given on Actual Size
Pattern Sheet Side A.

40 cm
(15 3/4″)

34.5 cm
(13 5/8″)

(13 5/8″) 34.5 cm

12.5 cm
(4 7/8″)

(7 1/16″)

18 cm Attach pocket
here.

12.5 cm
(4 7/8″)

9 cm
(3 1/2″)

12.5 cm

11 cm
(4 3/8″)

40 cm

(4 3/4″)
12 cm

(4 7/8″)
12.5 cm

12.5 cm

20 cm

23 cm
(9 1/16″)

(14 5/8″) 37 cm

Actual size patterns for
small bag is given on same
pattern sheet. Directions
given for large bag also
apply to samll bag.

(Directions)

(1) Make templates.
(2) Cut pieces adding 1 cm (3/8″) seam allowance.

Trace quilting lines for left and right panels
and heart applique placement lines. Place
background fabric on tracing paper and trace
quilting lines and heart applique placement
lines with sharp 2B pencil.

Seam allowance
5 mm (1/4″)

Mark hearts on right side
of fabric. Add 5 mm (1/4″)
seam allowance and cut.

(3) Applique hearts.
Pins and basting will not hold applique piece
securely.
Use glue or paste (regular kind that children
use).

Apply dots of glue on
wrong side of hearts.

Turning the edges with tip
of needle, blindstitch
piece to background fabric.

Clip

After blind-stitching to this point,
peel glue off with tip of needle.

Layer each section with batting and backing fabric. Baste.

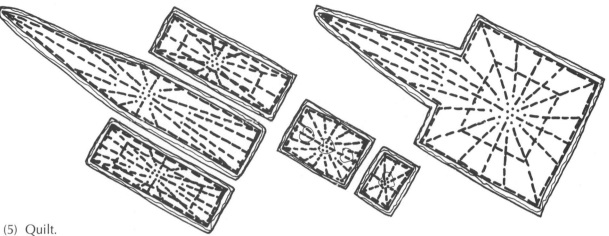

(5) Quilt.
   After quilting, apply patterns and mark finished lines.
   Trim seam allowance to same width.

(6) Bind opening with bias strip.

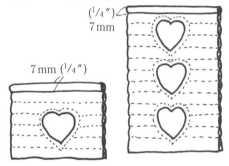

($^1/_4$")
7 mm

7 mm ($^1/_4$")

Place small pocket and baste around edges.

With right sides together, sew the bottom edge of large pocket, flip inside out and baste sides.

(7) Sew (6) and left and right panels together.
   With right sides together, sew front and back.

(8) Make lining bag.
   Cut lining fabric adding 7 mm ($^1/_4$") seam allowance. With right sides together, sew as shown in illustration, leaving a 12 cm (4$^3/_4$") opening.

Opening for turning 12 cm (4$^3/_4$")

Clip   Clip

(9) With right sides together, sew top edge of (7) and (8).
   Clip corners.

   (10) Turn inside out and sew opening. Tie ends in a cute bow.

* Stitch edges on the back to keep edges from curling. (Stitches should not show on front)

Scramble Pattern Shopping Bag and Pouch

I created this bag with whatever blocks and borders I had from my previous quilts. I added extra strips and entwined handles made from bias fabric. And voila! I have a new look to my shopping bag.

Instructions on pages 30, 31.

SHOPPING BAG & POUCH

MS.CHUCK'S
PATCHWORK
[pách'wûrk']

A kind of fancy work in which pieces of cloth differing in color and shape are sewn together,

oftentimes to form a design,

and which is used in covering quilts,

pillows, etc.; hence,

similarly variegated or checkered appearance or scene;

as a patchwork of fields.

Scramble Pattern Shopping Bag and Pouch .... PP. 28, 29

(Materials)
Assorted scraps of print fabric
Backing fabric, batting······120 cm × 50 cm
($47^1/4'' × 19^3/4''$)
Cardboard······40 cm × 15 cm ($15^3/4'' × 6''$)

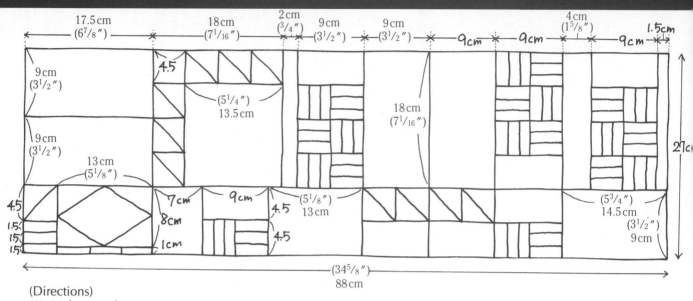

17.5cm ($6^7/8''$) — 18cm ($7^1/16''$) — 2cm ($3/4''$) 9cm ($3^1/2''$) — 9cm ($3^1/2''$) — 9cm — 9cm — 4cm ($1^5/8''$) — 9cm — 1.5cm

9cm ($3^1/2''$)
9cm ($3^1/2''$)
13cm ($5^1/8''$)
4.5
($5^1/4''$) 13.5cm
18cm ($7^1/16''$)
27c

4.5
1.5
1.5
1.5
7cm
8cm
1cm
9cm
4.5
4.5
($5^1/8''$) 13cm
($5^3/4''$) 14.5cm
($3^1/2''$) 9cm

($34^5/8''$)
88cm

(Directions)
(1) Make templates.
(2) Cut pieces adding 7mm ($1/4''$) seam allowance.

(3) Sew pieces together.

* Since there are many pieces, don't cut them all at the beginning. It will be easier if you sew a few blocks, check color coordination and then choose next fabric, cut and piece.

[Bottom]
Pattern for bottom section is on Actual Size Pattern Sheet Side A.

14.5 cm

($14^1/8''$)
36cm

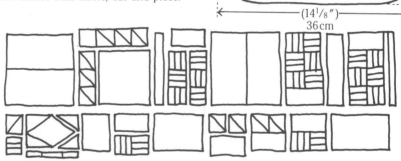

(4) Layer batting and backing fabric to (3). Baste.

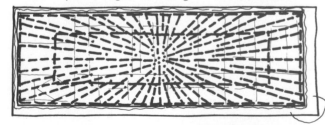

Allow more backing fabric on one side and bottom edge for binding seam allowance.

(5) Quilt.

(1.5cm ($5/8''$) wide quilting lines)

Layer and baste bottom section.

Bottom

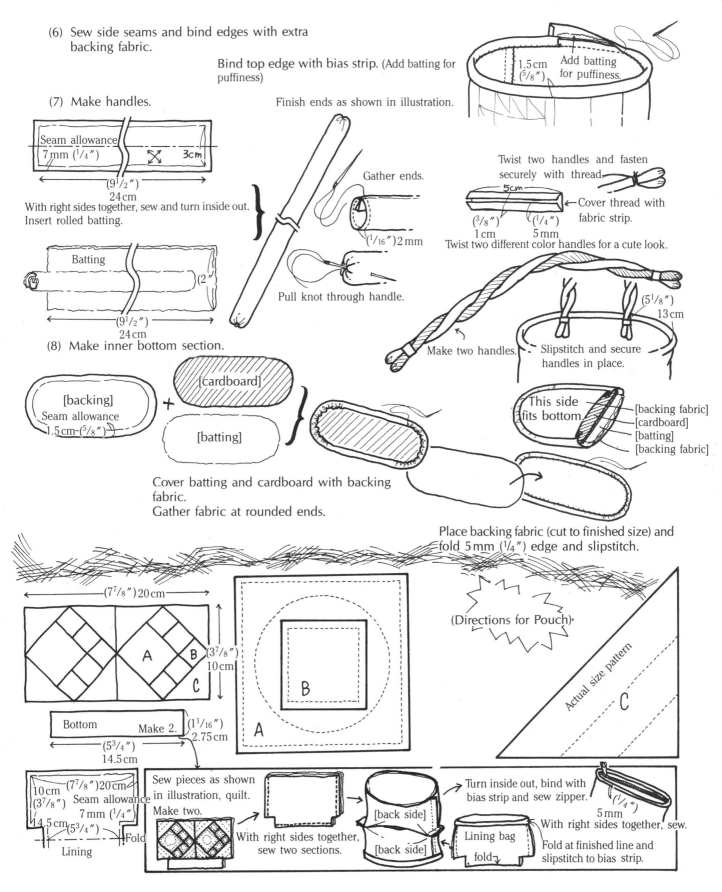

(6) Sew side seams and bind edges with extra backing fabric.

Bind top edge with bias strip. (Add batting for puffiness)

1.5cm (⁵/₈″) Add batting for puffiness.

(7) Make handles.

Finish ends as shown in illustration.

Seam allowance 7 mm (¹/₄″)   3cm

(9¹/₂″) 24cm

With right sides together, sew and turn inside out. Insert rolled batting.

Gather ends.

(¹/₁₆″)2mm

Pull knot through handle.

Twist two handles and fasten securely with thread.
←Cover thread with fabric strip.

5cm
(³/₈″) 1cm   (¹/₄″) 5mm

Twist two different color handles for a cute look.

Batting
(2″)

(9¹/₂″) 24cm

(8) Make inner bottom section.

[backing] Seam allowance 1.5cm-(⁵/₈″)

+ [cardboard]
[batting]

(5¹/₈″) 13cm

Make two handles.   Slipstitch and secure handles in place.

This side fits bottom.
[backing fabric]
[cardboard]
[batting]
[backing fabric]

Cover batting and cardboard with backing fabric.
Gather fabric at rounded ends.

Place backing fabric (cut to finished size) and fold 5mm (¹/₄″) edge and slipstitch.

(7⁷/₈″)20cm

A B C

(3⁷/₈″) 10cm

B

A

Bottom   Make 2.

(1¹/₁₆″) 2.75cm

(5³/₄″) 14.5cm

(Directions for Pouch)

Actual size pattern   C

10cm (3⁷/₈″)   (7⁷/₈″)20cm
Seam allowance 7 mm (¹/₄″)
14.5cm (5³/₄″)   Fold
Lining

Sew pieces as shown in illustration, quilt. Make two.

With right sides together, sew two sections.

[back side]

[back side]

Turn inside out, bind with bias strip and sew zipper.

(¹/₄″) 5mm

With right sides together, sew.

Lining bag
fold

Fold at finished line and slipstitch to bias strip.

OPERA BAG

Cathedral Window Opera Bag

The pattern is derived from the windows in churches. Customarily, white fabric is used for the background. However, by adapting background material as shown in the pictures, you get a very fashionable effect. This pattern calls for the folding technique and so the amount of background material is five times the finished size.

Instructions on pages 34, 35.

MS.CHUCK'S
PATCHWORK
[pách'wûrk']

A kind of fancy work in which pieces of cloth differing in color and shape are sewn together,

oftentimes to form a design,

and which is used in covering quilts,

pillows, etc.; hence,

a similarly variegated or checkered appearance or scene,

as a patchwork of fields.

Cathedral Window
Opera Bags .... PP. 32, 33

(Materials)
Background fabric ...... 130 cm × 80 cm
(51 1/4″ × 31 1/2″)
Lining fabric ...... 70 cm × 30 cm (27 1/2″ × 11 3/4″)
Assorted scraps of print fabric
Batting ...... 20 cm × 20 cm (7 7/8″ × 7 7/8″)
Cardboard ...... 20 cm × 20 cm (7 7/8″ × 7 7/8″)

(Directions)
Machine-piecing Method
(1) Cut required number squares adding 7 mm (1/4″) seam allowance.

(2) Sew both sides.

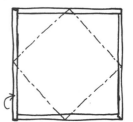

Seam allowance 7 mm (1/4″)

(3) With right sides together and seams aligned, sew, leaving 2.5 cm (1″) opening. Turn inside out and sew opening.

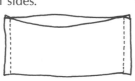

Opening about 2.5 cm (1″)

(4) Sew (3) as shown in illustration.

(5) Fold corners so that they meet in center and sew securely.

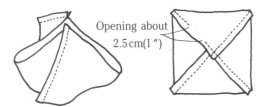

Basic Piecing Method
(1) Cut required number squares adding 7 mm (1/4″) seam allowance.

(2) Fold seam allowance.

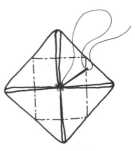

(3) Fold corners and sew at center.

(4) Turn over and fold corners, sew corners at center.

(5) With right sides together, whipstitch (4).

(6) Placing different squares of scrap fabric in the center, blindstitch edges.

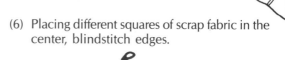

Cut four sides of scrap fabric in a curve. This will give a nice finish.

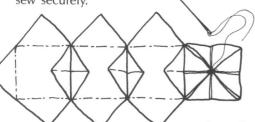

(1/8″) 3 mm

Start slipstitch from top of curve.

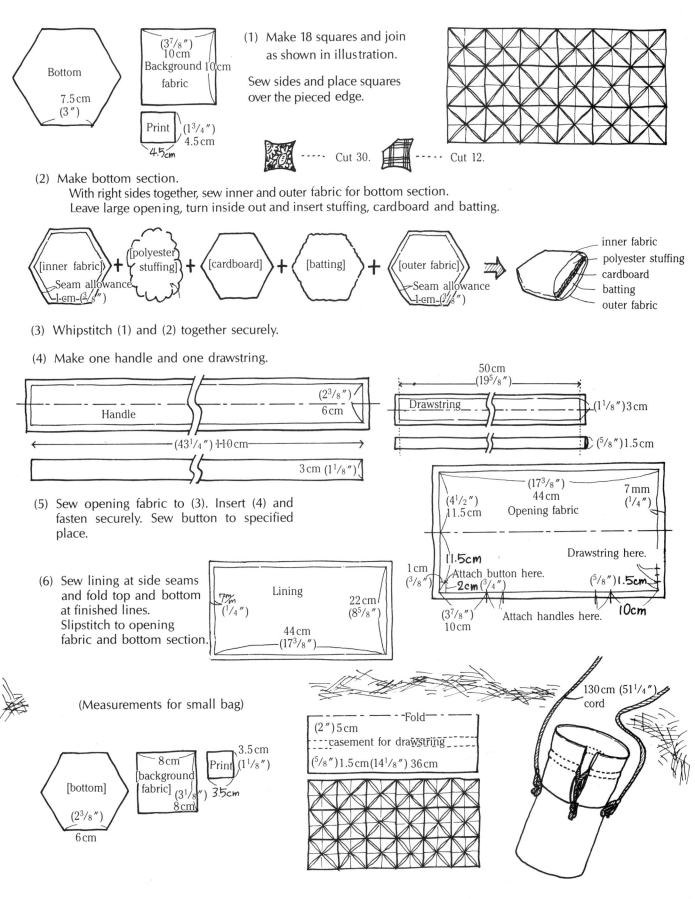

Bottom
7.5 cm
(3″)

($3^7/8$″)
10 cm
Background 10 cm
fabric

Print ($1^3/4$″)
4.5 cm
4.5 cm

(1) Make 18 squares and join as shown in illustration.

Sew sides and place squares over the pieced edge.

····· Cut 30.   ····· Cut 12.

(2) Make bottom section.
  With right sides together, sew inner and outer fabric for bottom section.
  Leave large opening, turn inside out and insert stuffing, cardboard and batting.

[inner fabric] + [polyester stuffing] + [cardboard] + [batting] + [outer fabric] ⇒

Seam allowance 1 cm ($3/8$″)

Seam allowance 1 cm ($3/8$″)

inner fabric
polyester stuffing
cardboard
batting
outer fabric

(3) Whipstitch (1) and (2) together securely.

(4) Make one handle and one drawstring.

Handle   ($2^3/8$″) 6 cm

($43^1/4$″) 110 cm

3 cm ($1^1/8$″)

50 cm
($19^5/8$″)

Drawstring   ($1^1/8$″) 3 cm

($5/8$″) 1.5 cm

(5) Sew opening fabric to (3). Insert (4) and fasten securely. Sew button to specified place.

($17^3/8$″)
44 cm

($4^1/2$″)
11.5 cm   Opening fabric

7 mm
($1/4$″)

11.5 cm

Drawstring here.

1 cm
($3/8$″)

Attach button here.
2 cm ($3/4$″)

($5/8$″) 1.5 cm

($3^7/8$″)
10 cm

Attach handles here.

10 cm

(6) Sew lining at side seams and fold top and bottom at finished lines.
  Slipstitch to opening fabric and bottom section.

Lining

7 mm
($1/4$″)

22 cm
($8^5/8$″)

44 cm
($17^3/8$″)

(Measurements for small bag)

[bottom]
($2^3/8$″)
6 cm

8 cm
[background fabric]
($3^1/8$″)
8 cm

Print ($1^1/8$″)
3.5 cm
3.5 cm

─ Fold ─
(2″) 5 cm
‒‒‒ casement for drawstring ‒‒‒
($5/8$″) 1.5 cm ($14^1/8$″) 36 cm

130 cm ($51^1/4$″) cord

35

Pieced Tulip Bags: Big and Small

Pieced tulips placed on the diagonal with a dark background create a sophisticated bag. School girls and children love little shoulder bags! Wouldn't this be a superb birthday present? It is surprising how much it can hold.

Instructions on pages 38, 39.

MS. CHUCK'S
PATCHWORK
[pách'wûrk']

A kind of fancy work in which pieces of cloth differing in color and shape are sewn together,

oftentimes to form a design,

and which is used in covering quilts,

pillows, etc.; hence,

a similarly variegated or checkered appearance or scene,

as a patchwork of fields.

PRETTY POCHETTE

(Materials)
Background fabric, backing fabric, batting
⋯⋯1 m × 50 cm ($39^3/_8$″ × $19^3/_4$″) each
Assorted scraps of print fabric

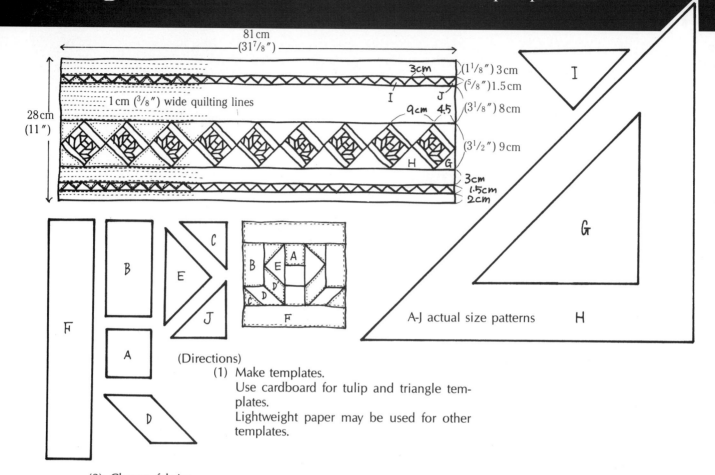

81cm
($31^7/_8$″)

28cm
(11″)

3cm
($1^1/_8$″) 3cm
($5/_8$″) 1.5 cm
1 cm ($3/_8$″) wide quilting lines
I J
9cm 4.5 ($3^1/_8$″) 8cm
($3^1/_2$″) 9cm
H G
3cm
1.5cm
2cm

I

G

A-J actual size patterns   H

F   B   C   E   J   A   D

B   E   A
E
D
C D
F

(Directions)

(1) Make templates.
Use cardboard for tulip and triangle templates.
Lightweight paper may be used for other templates.

(2) Choose fabrics.
Cut pieces adding following seam allowances:
tulip pieces⋯⋯5 mm ($1/_4$″)
triangles⋯⋯7 mm ($1/_4$″)
other pieces⋯⋯1 cm ($3/_8$″)

Arrange all pieces in order and check color coordination.

(3) Sew pieces together.

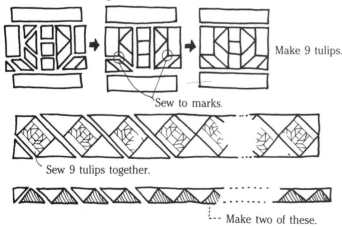

Make 9 tulips.

Sew to marks.

Sew 9 tulips together.

Make two of these.

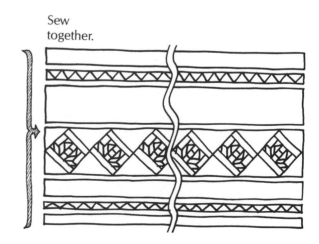

Sew together.

(4) Draw quilting lines with sharp 2B pencil.
Layer with batting and backing fabric. Baste.

Always baste from center outwards and get those wrinkles out!

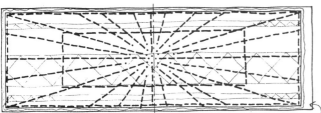

Cut backing fabric larger than batting or pieced section. It will be used to bind seam allowance.

Layer bottom section in the same way and baste.

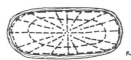

For bottom section pattern, look at Actual Size Pattern Sheet Side A.

(5) Quilt.

(6) Sew side seams of pieced section. Bind seam allowance with backing fabric.

Bind opening with bias strip.

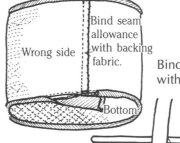

Wrong side

Bind seam allowance with backing fabric.

Bottom

Bind seam allowance with bias strip.

(7) With right sides together, sew (6) and bottom section.
Distribute excess fabric evenly.

After quilting, everybody has that little extra! Don't worry.

12cm (4³/₈″) (2¹/₈″) 5.5cm↗ 12cm

Slipstitch securely in place.

(8) Make handles.

50cm

Cut 2.

(2³/₄″)
↓7cm

Seam allowance 0.7cm (¹/₄″)

3.5cm

50cm (19⁵/₈″)

Batting cut 2.

10cm (3⁷/₈″)

The back section can be quilted like this!

(Measurements for small bag)

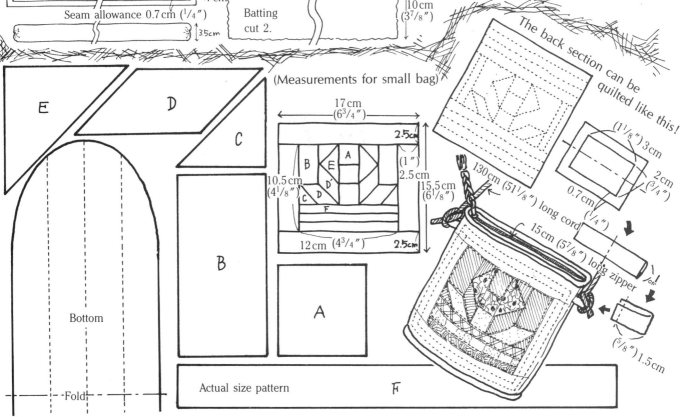

E   D

C

17cm (6³/₄″)

2.5cm

B   A

(1″) 2.5cm

E

10.5cm (4¹/₈″)

D′
C   D
F

15.5cm (6¹/₈″)

12cm (4³/₄″)   2.5cm

(1¹/₈″) 3cm

2cm (³/₄″)

0.7cm (¹/₄″)

130cm (51¹/₈″) long cord

15cm (5⁷/₈″) long zipper

(⁵/₈″) 1.5cm

B

Bottom

Fold

A

Actual size pattern   F

Gorgeous Satin Gift Bags

Anyone would want a present in this lovely gift bag, so easy and quick to make. The bag itself is a present and any receiver will cherish it. It is embellished with a house, hexagon flowers, stars, or baskets and an extra personal touch would be to embroider his or her initials or a commemorative date on the back.

Instructions on pages 42, 43.

WRAPPING CASE

MS.CHUCK'S
PATCHWORK
[pách'wûrk']

A kind of fancy work in which pieces of cloth differing in color and shape are sewn together,

oftentimes to form a design,

and which is used in covering quilts,

pillows, etc.; hence,

a similarly variegated or checkered appearance or scene,

as a patchwork of fields.

Gorgeous Satin Gift Bags

·······························PP. 40, 41

(Materials)
Fabric for bags
Assorted scraps of print fabric
#25 Embroidery floss
Ribbon······1 m (39³/₈″)

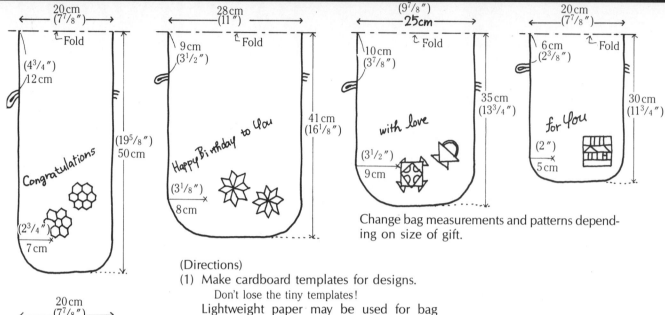

Change bag measurements and patterns depending on size of gift.

(Directions)
(1) Make cardboard templates for designs.
    Don't lose the tiny templates!
    Lightweight paper may be used for bag pattern.

(2) Choose fabric for bag and designs, checking for color coordination.
    Cut pieces adding 7 mm (¹/₄″) seam allowance.
    Arrange design pieces on bag fabric and check the colors.

(3) Sew pieces together and applique on bag.

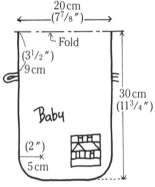

Patterns for 5 designs that are given here are all actual size.

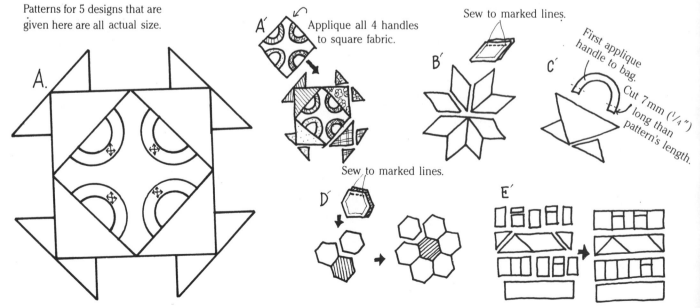

(4) Embroider messages with 3 strands of embroidery floss.

Use outline stitch.
Messages are on Actual Size Pattern Sheet Side A.

Outline stitch

3 out
2 in
1 out

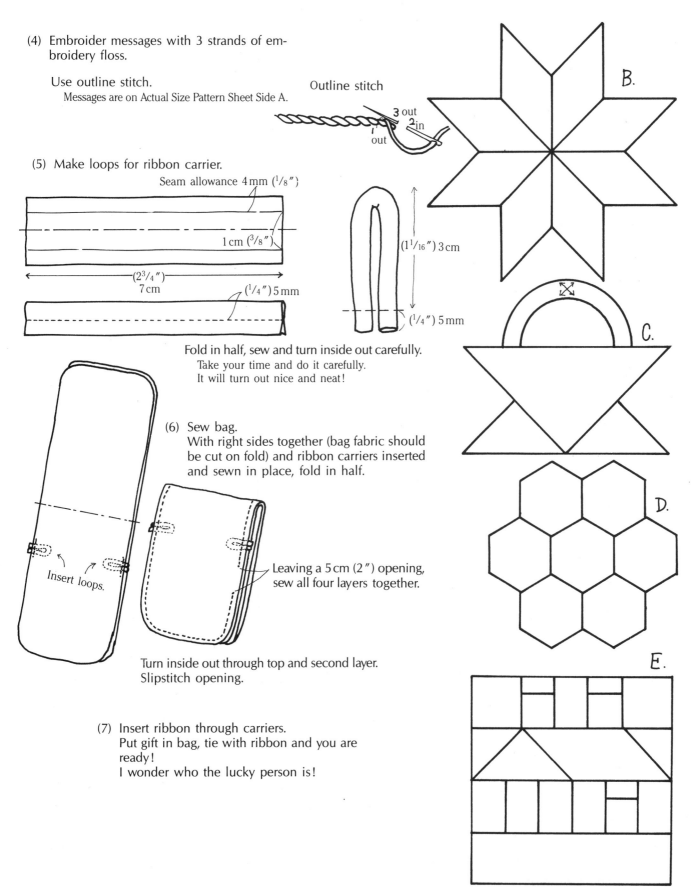

B.

(5) Make loops for ribbon carrier.

Seam allowance 4 mm (¹/₈″)

1 cm (³/₈″)

(2³/₄″)
7 cm

(¹/₄″) 5 mm

(1¹/₁₆″) 3 cm

(¹/₄″) 5 mm

C.

Fold in half, sew and turn inside out carefully.
Take your time and do it carefully.
It will turn out nice and neat!

(6) Sew bag.
With right sides together (bag fabric should be cut on fold) and ribbon carriers inserted and sewn in place, fold in half.

D.

Insert loops.

Leaving a 5 cm (2″) opening, sew all four layers together.

Turn inside out through top and second layer.
Slipstitch opening.

E.

(7) Insert ribbon through carriers.
Put gift in bag, tie with ribbon and you are ready!
I wonder who the lucky person is!

The secret of this bag is the hooked bottom. The border patterns are often used in lattices of bed quilts. Hook the bottom, and you have a new look and more room.

Instructions on pages 46, 47.

Hooked Bags with Pattern and Style Variations

Hooked Bags with Pattern and Style Variations·····PP. 44, 45

(Materials)
Background fabric·····1 m × 60 cm (39³/₈″ × 23¹/₂″)
Assorted scraps of print fabric
Backing fabric, batting·····1 m × 50 cm (39³/₈″ × 19³/₄″) each
1 Hook

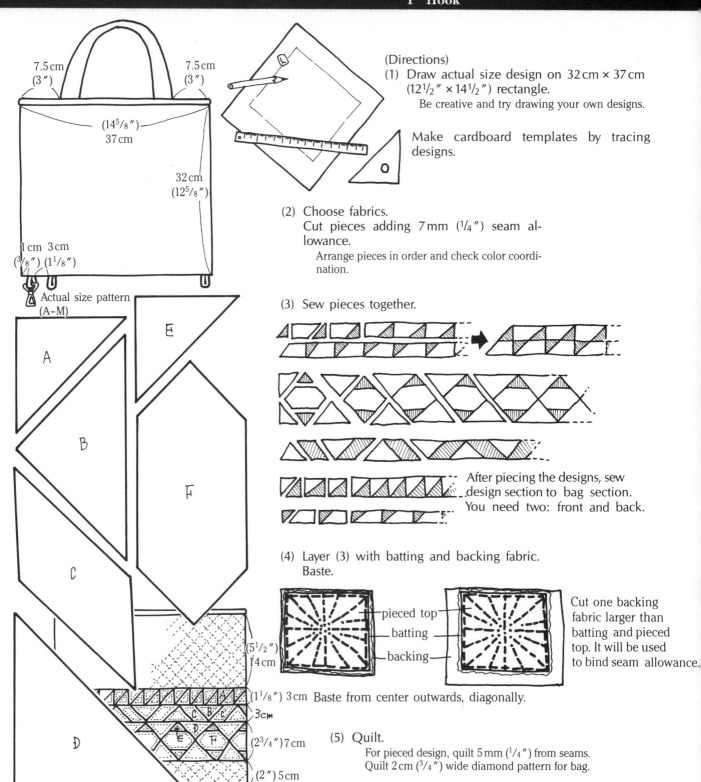

7.5 cm (3″)   7.5 cm (3″)

(14⁵/₈″) 37 cm

32 cm (12⁵/₈″)

1 cm 3 cm (³/₈″) (1¹/₈″)

Actual size pattern (A–M)

A

B

C

D

E

F

(5¹/₂″) 14 cm

(1¹/₈″) 3 cm

3 cm

(2³/₄″) 7 cm

(2″) 5 cm

(Directions)
(1) Draw actual size design on 32 cm × 37 cm (12¹/₂″ × 14¹/₂″) rectangle.

 Be creative and try drawing your own designs.

 Make cardboard templates by tracing designs.

(2) Choose fabrics.
 Cut pieces adding 7 mm (¹/₄″) seam allowance.

  Arrange pieces in order and check color coordination.

(3) Sew pieces together.

After piecing the designs, sew design section to bag section.
You need two: front and back.

(4) Layer (3) with batting and backing fabric. Baste.

pieced top
batting
backing

Cut one backing fabric larger than batting and pieced top. It will be used to bind seam allowance.

Baste from center outwards, diagonally.

(5) Quilt.
 For pieced design, quilt 5 mm (¹/₄″) from seams.
 Quilt 2 cm (³/₄″) wide diamond pattern for bag.

(6) Make hook loop.

With right sides together, sew bias strip and turn inside out. Insert yarn and fold in half.

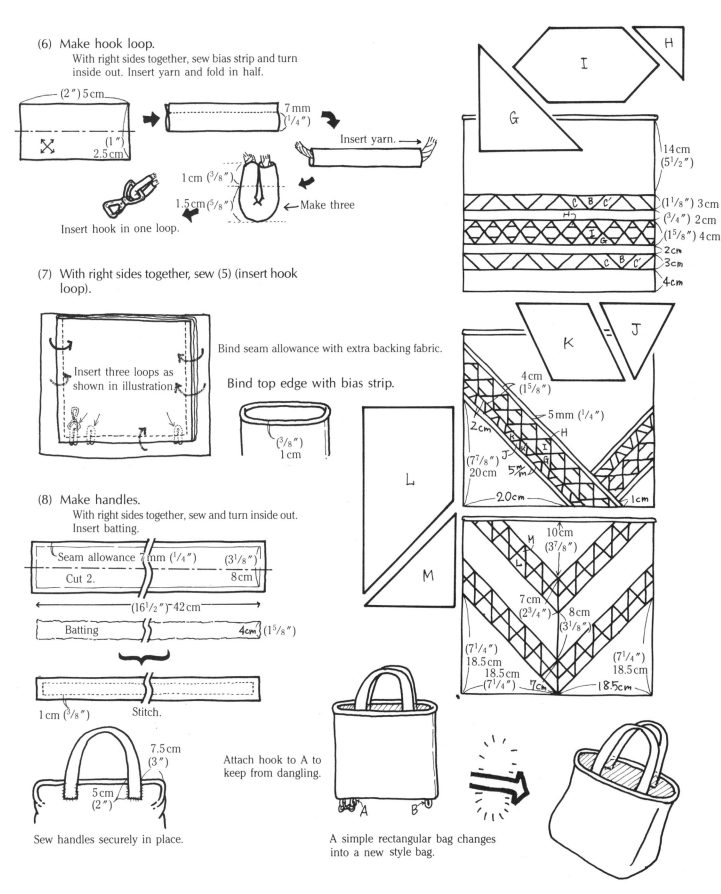

(2″) 5 cm

7 mm (¼″)

(1″) 2.5 cm

Insert yarn.

1 cm (³/₈″)

1.5 cm (⁵/₈″) ← Make three

Insert hook in one loop.

(7) With right sides together, sew (5) (insert hook loop).

Insert three loops as shown in illustration.

Bind seam allowance with extra backing fabric.

Bind top edge with bias strip.

(³/₈″) 1 cm

(8) Make handles.

With right sides together, sew and turn inside out. Insert batting.

Seam allowance 7 mm (¼″)   (3¹/₈″)

Cut 2.   8 cm

(16¹/₂″) 42 cm

Batting   4 cm (1⁵/₈″)

1 cm (³/₈″)   Stitch.

7.5 cm (3″)

5 cm (2″)

Sew handles securely in place.

Attach hook to A to keep from dangling.

A simple rectangular bag changes into a new style bag.

G   H   I

14 cm (5¹/₂″)

(1¹/₈″) 3 cm
(³/₄″) 2 cm
(1⁵/₈″) 4 cm
2 cm
3 cm
4 cm

C B C′
H
I G
C B C′

J   K

4 cm (1⁵/₈″)

5 mm (¼″)

2 cm   H

L

(7⁷/₈″) 20 cm   5 mm

20 cm   1 cm

J I G

10 cm (3⁷/₈″)

M   L

7 cm (2³/₄″)

8 cm (3¹/₈″)

(7¹/₄″) 18.5 cm   18.5 cm   (7¹/₄″) 18.5 cm

(7¹/₄″)   7 cm   18.5 cm

A   B

Colorful Dogwood Cosmetic Cases

I have used the dogwood pattern for this cosmetic case. Why is it called dogwood? Because if you look at the petals closely, it looks just like the dark tip of a dog's nose. The Japanese call this flower Hanamizuki. The petals are turned up and stuffed and sharp triangles are placed between the petals to set off the flower. There is a round bottom and by adding straps, it can be used as a shoulder bag.

Instructions on pages 50, 51.

MAKE UP POUCH

MS.CHUCK'S
PATCHWORK
[pách'wûrk']

A kind of fancy work in which pieces of cloth differing in color and shape are sewn together,

oftentimes to form a design,

and which is used in covering quilts,

pillows, etc.; hence,

a motley variegated or checkered appearance or scene;

a great number of fields

Colorful Dogwood
Cosmetic Cases······ PP. 48, 49

(Materials)
Background fabric, backing fabric, batting
······**70 cm × 15 cm (27¹/₂″ × 6″) each**
 # 25 Embroidery floss
1 20 cm (7⁷/₈″) zipper

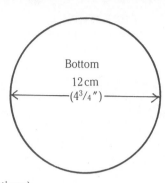

Bottom
12 cm
(4³/₄″)

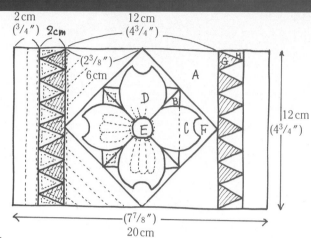

2 cm (³/₄″) 2cm 12cm (4³/₄″)

(2³/₈″)
6 cm

A
D B
C F
E

12cm (4³/₄″)

(7⁷/₈″)
20 cm

(Directions)
(1) Make cardboard templates.
(2) Cut pieces adding 7 mm (¹/₄″) seam allowance.
> Arrange pieces in order and check color coordination.
> Change any pieces that look out of place.

(3) Sew pieces together.
> It's fun sewing the center dogwood piece!

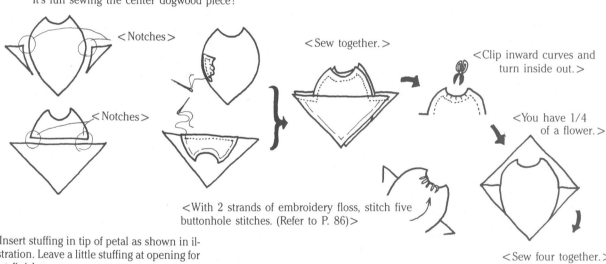

< Notches >

< Notches >

< Sew together. >

< Clip inward curves and turn inside out. >

< You have 1/4 of a flower. >

< With 2 strands of embroidery floss, stitch five buttonhole stitches. (Refer to P. 86) >

< Sew four together. >

< Insert stuffing in tip of petal as shown in illustration. Leave a little stuffing at opening for neat finish. >

< Insert polyester stuffing into petals for puffiness. >

< Applique center circle. >

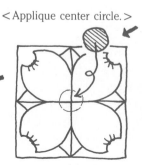

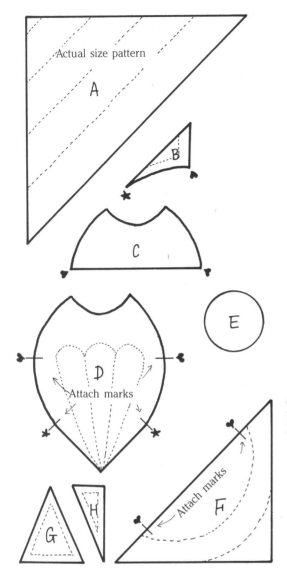

Actual size pattern

A

B

C

E

D

Attach marks

G

H

F

Attach marks

<Piece triangles.>

·····<Make 2.>

<Piece together.>

(4) Draw quilting lines with a sharp 2B pencil. Layer pieced top with batting and backing fabric. Baste.

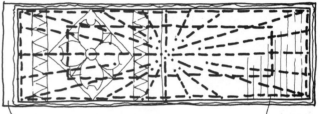

Cut backing fabric larger than pieced top and batting.
It will be used to bind seam allowance.

Draw 1 cm ($^3/_8$″) wide quilting lines on back.

(5) Quilt. (Refer P.6)

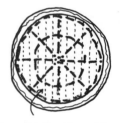

1 cm ($^3/_8$″) wide quilting line.

(6) Sew side seams. Bind seam allowance with extra backing fabric.

Bind top edge with bias strip.

Wrong side

(7) With right sides together, sew (6) and bottom section together. (Ease in excess fabric) Bind seam allowance with bias strip.

(8) Hand-sew zipper.

Corners of zipper should look like this.

Fold corners.

Do a catch-stitch.

51

Easy Pattern Coin Purses

These are all very easy-to-make coin purses for beginning quilters. Make one and you can't stop making more.

Instructions on page 55.

SMALL CHANGE PURSE

Strip-quilted Tote Bag and Purse

This is a darling bag with lots of room. Choose the shape of purse to match on your mood.

Instructions on page 54.

(Materials)
Background fabric······120 cm × 60 cm
($47\frac{1}{4}'' \times 23\frac{1}{2}''$)
Backing fabric, batting······120 cm × 50 cm
($47\frac{1}{4}'' \times 19\frac{3}{4}''$)
Assorted scraps of print fabric
Lining fabric······1 m × 30 cm ($39\frac{3}{8}'' \times 11\frac{3}{4}''$)

(Directions)
(1) Prepare 6 triangles with backing fabric. (Using old sheets is a good idea!)
Cut 6 triangles from batting. Layer backing fabric and batting. Baste.

<1 cm seam allowance>
\<backing fabric\>

+

\<batting\>
Make 6.

=

Make basting knots on backing fabric side for easy removal.

Make 6.

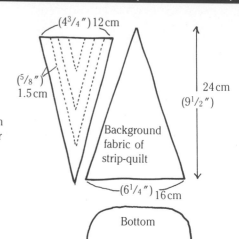

($4\frac{3}{4}''$) 12 cm

($\frac{5}{8}''$) 1.5 cm

Background fabric of strip-quilt

24 cm
($9\frac{1}{2}''$)

($6\frac{1}{4}''$) 16 cm

Bottom

Patterns are given on Actual size pattern sheet side A.

(2) Strip-quilt.

Always keep color coordination in mind.

Place 1st strip.
Place 2nd strip, right sides together and sew all layers. (You are strip-piecing and quilting at the same time so take nice tiny stitches!)
Flip open and crease.
Repeat the previous procedure till you have covered the triangle.
Use different width strips. The strips may be pieced.

(3) Layer large triangle with batting and backing fabric.

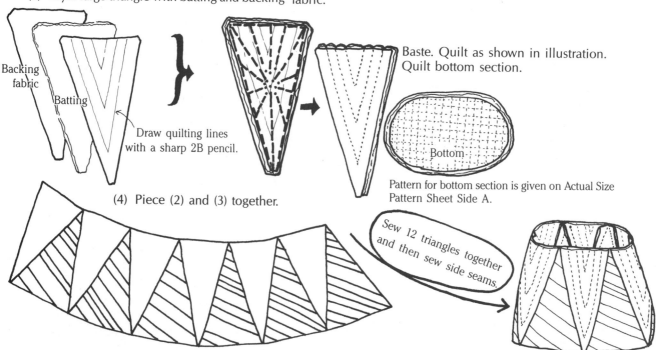

Backing fabric

Batting

Draw quilting lines with a sharp 2B pencil.

Baste. Quilt as shown in illustration. Quilt bottom section.

Bottom

Pattern for bottom section is given on Actual Size Pattern Sheet Side A.

(4) Piece (2) and (3) together.

Sew 12 triangles together and then sew side seams.

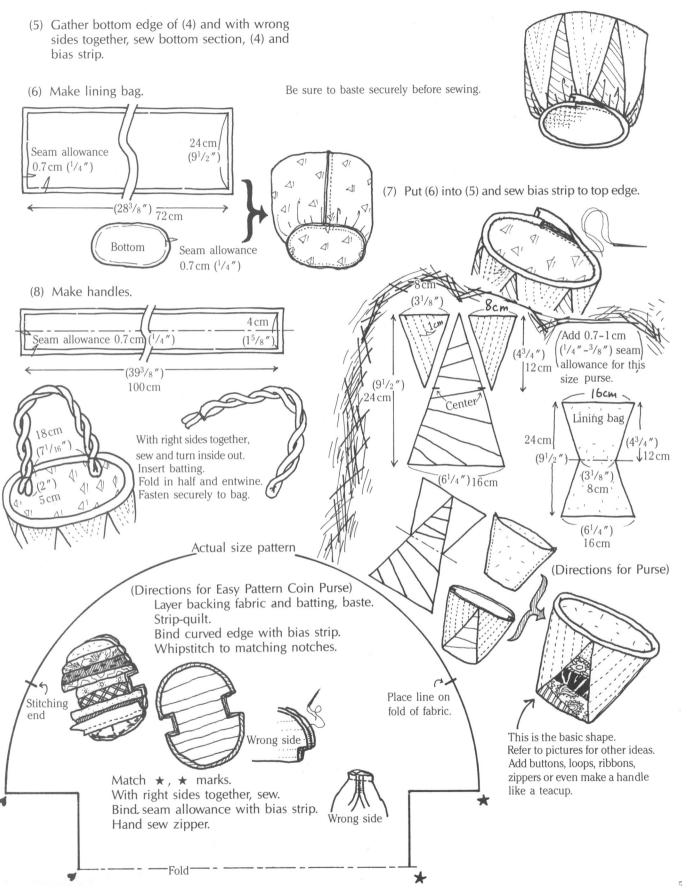

(5) Gather bottom edge of (4) and with wrong sides together, sew bottom section, (4) and bias strip.

(6) Make lining bag.

Be sure to baste securely before sewing.

Seam allowance 0.7cm (¹/₄″)

24cm (9¹/₂″)

(28³/₈″) 72cm

Bottom

Seam allowance 0.7cm (¹/₄″)

(7) Put (6) into (5) and sew bias strip to top edge.

8cm (3¹/₈″)

8cm

1cm

(4³/₄″) 12cm

Add 0.7–1cm (¹/₄″–³/₈″) seam allowance for this size purse.

(9¹/₂″) 24cm

Center

(6¹/₄″)16cm

16cm

Lining bag

24cm (9¹/₂″)

(4³/₄″) ↓12cm

(3¹/₈″) 8cm

(6¹/₄″) 16cm

(Directions for Purse)

(8) Make handles.

4cm (1⁵/₈″)

Seam allowance 0.7cm (¹/₄″)

(39³/₈″) 100cm

18cm (7¹/₁₆″)

(2″) 5cm

With right sides together, sew and turn inside out. Insert batting. Fold in half and entwine. Fasten securely to bag.

Actual size pattern

(Directions for Easy Pattern Coin Purse)
Layer backing fabric and batting, baste.
Strip-quilt.
Bind curved edge with bias strip.
Whipstitch to matching notches.

Stitching end

Wrong side

Place line on fold of fabric.

Match ★ , ★ marks.
With right sides together, sew.
Bind seam allowance with bias strip.
Hand sew zipper.

Wrong side

This is the basic shape.
Refer to pictures for other ideas.
Add buttons, loops, ribbons, zippers or even make a handle like a teacup.

Fold

★

★

Sundial D-Bag and Heart-tree Appliqued Knapsack

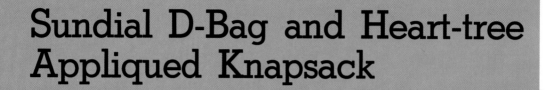

These bags are the most challenging in this book. But wouldn't it be nice to walk the streets with one of these fashionable bags on your back? I would be so happy that I wouldn't be able to keep my eyes off one!

Instructions on pages 58, 59.

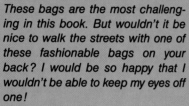

MS.CHUCK'S
PATCHWORK
[pách'wûrk']

A kind of fancy work in which pieces of cloth differing in color and shape are sewn together,

oftentimes to form a design,

and which is used in covering quilts,

pillows, etc.; hence,

a similarly variegated or checkered appearance or scene,

as a patchwork of fields.

TOWN RUCK

Sundial D-Bag .... P. 56

(Materials)
Background fabric, backing fabric, batting
······90 cm × 80 cm (35 1/2″ × 31 1/2″)
Assorted scraps of print fabric
1 60 cm (23 1/2″) Zipper
Belt (2.5 cm (1″) wide)······120 cm (47 1/4″)
2 Hooks   Polyester stuffing

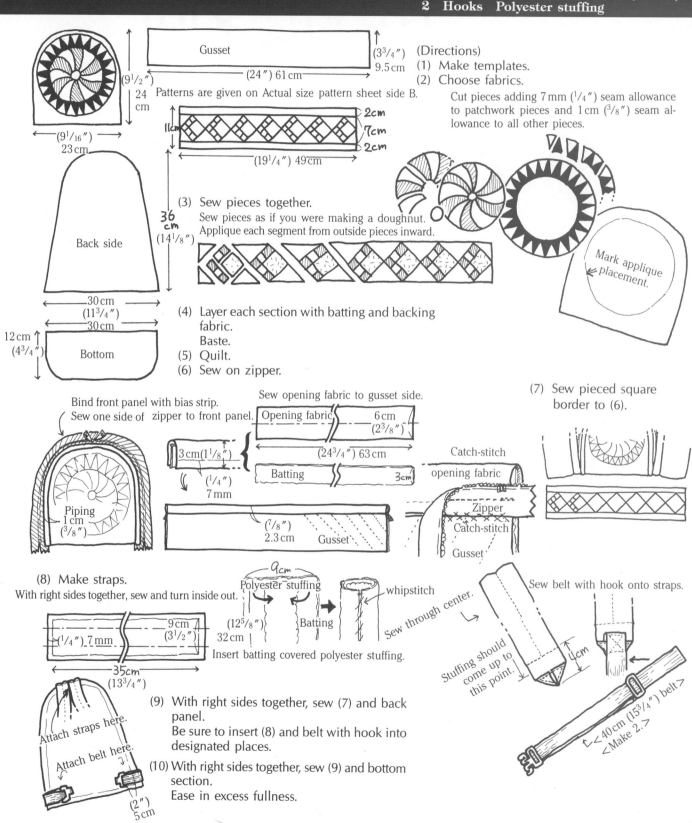

(Directions)
(1) Make templates.
(2) Choose fabrics.

Patterns are given on Actual size pattern sheet side B.

Cut pieces adding 7 mm (1/4″) seam allowance to patchwork pieces and 1 cm (3/8″) seam allowance to all other pieces.

Gusset (3 3/4″) 9.5 cm — (24″) 61 cm

(9 1/2″) 24 cm

(9 1/16″) 23 cm

2cm 7cm 2cm 11cm (19 1/4″) 49cm

Back side

36 cm (14 1/8″)

(3) Sew pieces together.
Sew pieces as if you were making a doughnut.
Applique each segment from outside pieces inward.

Mark applique placement.

30 cm (11 3/4″)
30 cm
12 cm (4 3/4″)
Bottom

(4) Layer each section with batting and backing fabric.
Baste.
(5) Quilt.
(6) Sew on zipper.

(7) Sew pieced square border to (6).

Bind front panel with bias strip.
Sew one side of zipper to front panel.

Sew opening fabric to gusset side.

Opening fabric 6 cm (2 3/8″)
3 cm (1 1/8″)
(1/4″) 7 mm
(24 3/4″) 63 cm
Batting 3 cm
(7/8″) 2.3 cm Gusset

Piping 1 cm (3/8″)

Catch-stitch
opening fabric
Zipper
Catch-stitch
Gusset

(8) Make straps.
With right sides together, sew and turn inside out.

9 cm
Polyester stuffing
whipstitch
(12 5/8″) 32 cm
Batting
Sew through center.
Insert batting covered polyester stuffing.

Sew belt with hook onto straps.
Stuffing should come up to this point.
4 cm
< 40 cm (15 3/4″) belt >
< Make 2. >

9 cm (3 1/2″)
(1/4″) 7 mm
35cm (13 3/4″)

Attach straps here.
Attach belt here.
(2″) 5 cm

(9) With right sides together, sew (7) and back panel.
Be sure to insert (8) and belt with hook into designated places.

(10) With right sides together, sew (9) and bottom section.
Ease in excess fullness.

Front panel fabric (small flower print)······80 cm × 60 cm
(31¹/₂″ × 23¹/₂″)
Backing fabric, batting······80 cm × 80 cm (31¹/₂″ × 31¹/₂″) square
Assorted scraps of print fabric
Lining fabric······130 cm × 50 cm (51¹/₄″ × 19³/₄″)
Velcro tape······4 cm (1¹/₂″)
Fusible interfacing······1 m × 10 cm (39³/₈″ × 4″)*

(Materials)
Front panel fabric (white)······1 m × 70 cm
(39³/₈″ × 27¹/₂″)

(Directions)
(1) Applique front panel
    (refer to P. 94).

For stem, use two (1.5 cm (⁵/₈″)
wide × 15 cm (6″) long) bias tape.

Stuff hearts and tulips with
polyester stuffing for puffiness.

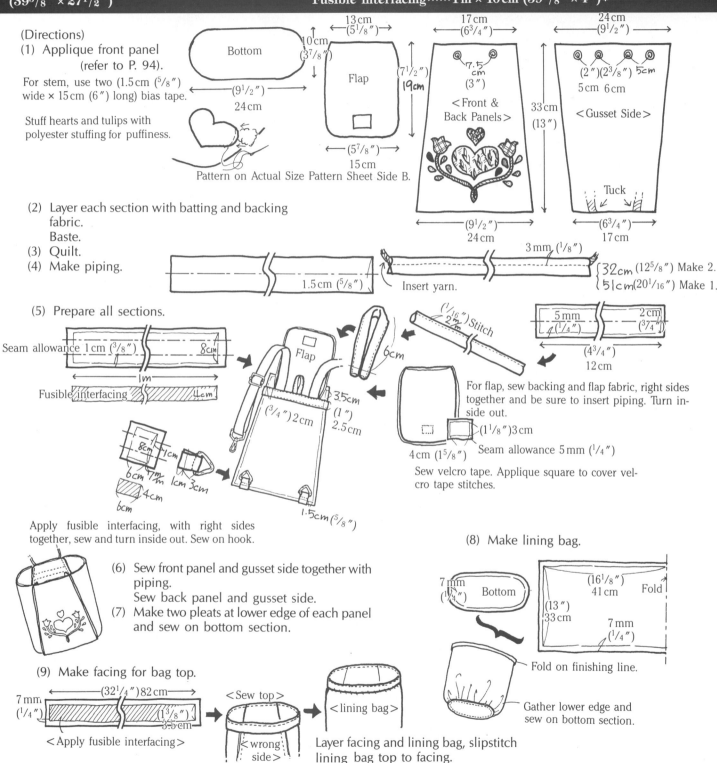

Pattern on Actual Size Pattern Sheet Side B.

(2) Layer each section with batting and backing
    fabric.
    Baste.
(3) Quilt.
(4) Make piping.

(5) Prepare all sections.

For flap, sew backing and flap fabric, right sides
together and be sure to insert piping. Turn inside out.

Seam allowance 5 mm (¹/₄″)

Sew velcro tape. Applique square to cover velcro tape stitches.

Apply fusible interfacing, with right sides
together, sew and turn inside out. Sew on hook.

(6) Sew front panel and gusset side together with
    piping.
    Sew back panel and gusset side.
(7) Make two pleats at lower edge of each panel
    and sew on bottom section.

(8) Make lining bag.

Fold on finishing line.

Gather lower edge and
sew on bottom section.

(9) Make facing for bag top.

Layer facing and lining bag, slipstitch
lining bag top to facing.

(10) Attach hammer-on snaps and insert ribbon.

* Ribbon······1 m (39³/₈″)
12   2 cm (³/₄″) diameter Hammer-on snaps
2   Hooks

Black and White Bag Set

I have used synthetic leather on the sides but it is not that difficult to handle. Use the bags as a pair or use them separately. You will have a long line of admirers.

Instructions on pages 62, 63.

61

Black and White Bag

.... **P. 60**

(Materials)
Leather······1 m × 60 cm (39³⁄₈″ × 23¹⁄₂″)
Assorted scraps of print fabric
Background fabric, batting······60 cm × 40 cm (23¹⁄₂″ × 15³⁄₄″) each
Lining fabric······150 cm × 40 cm (59″ × 15³⁄₄″) 1 Snap button

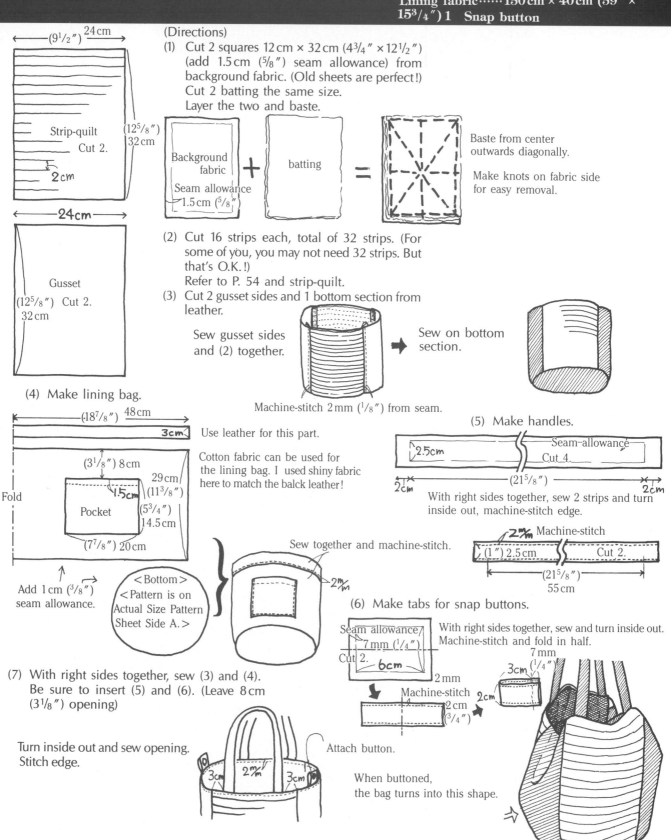

(Directions)

(1) Cut 2 squares 12 cm × 32 cm (4³⁄₄″ × 12¹⁄₂″) (add 1.5 cm (⁵⁄₈″) seam allowance) from background fabric. (Old sheets are perfect!) Cut 2 batting the same size. Layer the two and baste.

(9¹⁄₂″) 24 cm

Strip-quilt
Cut 2.

(12⁵⁄₈″) 32 cm

2 cm

Background fabric

Seam allowance 1.5 cm (⁵⁄₈″)

+ batting =

Baste from center outwards diagonally.

Make knots on fabric side for easy removal.

24 cm

Gusset
(12⁵⁄₈″) Cut 2.
32 cm

(2) Cut 16 strips each, total of 32 strips. (For some of you, you may not need 32 strips. But that's O.K.!) Refer to P. 54 and strip-quilt.

(3) Cut 2 gusset sides and 1 bottom section from leather.

Sew gusset sides and (2) together.

Sew on bottom section.

Machine-stitch 2 mm (¹⁄₈″) from seam.

(4) Make lining bag.

(18⁷⁄₈″) 48 cm

3 cm

Use leather for this part.

Cotton fabric can be used for the lining bag. I used shiny fabric here to match the balck leather!

(3¹⁄₈″) 8 cm
29 cm (11³⁄₈″)
1.5 cm
Pocket
(5³⁄₄″) 14.5 cm
(7⁷⁄₈″) 20 cm

Fold

Add 1 cm (³⁄₈″) seam allowance.

<Bottom> <Pattern is on Actual Size Pattern Sheet Side A.>

Sew together and machine-stitch.

2 mm

(5) Make handles.

2.5 cm
Seam-allowance Cut 4.
2 cm (21⁵⁄₈″) 2 cm

With right sides together, sew 2 strips and turn inside out, machine-stitch edge.

2 mm Machine-stitch
(1″) 2.5 cm Cut 2.
(21⁵⁄₈″) 55 cm

(6) Make tabs for snap buttons.

Seam allowance 7 mm (¹⁄₄″)
Cut 2.
6 cm
2 mm
Machine-stitch 2 cm (³⁄₄″)

With right sides together, sew and turn inside out. Machine-stitch and fold in half.

7 mm
3 cm (¹⁄₄″)
2 cm

(7) With right sides together, sew (3) and (4). Be sure to insert (5) and (6). (Leave 8 cm (3¹⁄₈″) opening)

Turn inside out and sew opening. Stitch edge.

3 cm 2 mm 3 cm

Attach button.

When buttoned, the bag turns into this shape.

Black and White Bag

•• P. 61

(Materials)
Assorted scraps of print fabric
Leather······50 cm × 25 cm (19³/₄″ × 9⁷/₈″)
Background fabric, batting······25 cm ×
25 cm (9⁷/₈″ × 9⁷/₈″) square each
1 20 cm (7⁷/₈″) Zipper
2 Cords······120 cm (47¹/₄″)

(Directions)

(1) Cut one background fabric and one batting. Layer and baste.

Background fabric

batting

Seam allowance 1 cm (³/₈″)

1.5 cm
(⁵/₈″)

(7¹/₁₆″)
18 cm

(8⁵/₈″) 22 cm

Width of strips is 1.5 cm (⁵/₈″). Add 7 mm (¹/₄″) seam allowance.

(2) Refer to P. 54 and strip-quilt.

(3) Cut back panel and bottom section from leather.
Cut batting and backing fabric. Layer the three and baste edged.

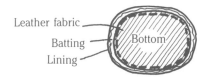

Leather fabric
Batting
Lining

Bottom

Backing fabric

Bottom

Pattern for bottom section ↗
Actual Size Pattern Sheet Side A.

Cut backing fabric larger on both sides.
It will be used to bind seam allowance.

(4) Make piping.

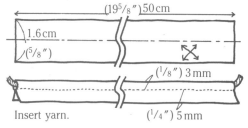

(19⁵/₈″) 50 cm

1.6 cm
(⁵/₈″)

(¹/₈″) 3 mm

Insert yarn.

(¹/₄″) 5 mm

(5) Make cord carriers.

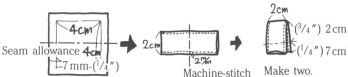

4 cm

Seam allowance 4 cm
7 mm-(¹/₄″)

2 cm

2 cm

2 cm

Machine-stitch

2 cm
(³/₄″) 2 cm
(¹/₄″) 7 cm

Make two.

(6) Insert (5) and sew the sections together.

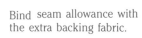

Bind seam allowance with the extra backing fabric.

2 cm
(³/₄″)

(7) Insert piping and sew (6) and bottom section.

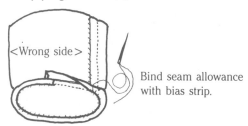

<Wrong side>

Bind seam allowance with bias strip.

(8) Bind top with bias strip and hand-sew zipper. Entwine two cords, insert through carriers and tie.

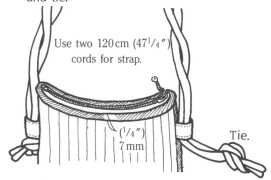

Use two 120 cm (47¹/₄″) cords for strap.

(¹/₄″)
7 mm

Tie.

MS.CHUCK'S
PATCHWORK
[pách'wûrk']

A kind of fancy work in which pieces of cloth differing in color and shape are sewed together,

oftentimes to form a design,

and which is used in covering bags,

pillows, etc.; a piece

a similarly variegated or checkered appearance; often

as a patchwork.

Dresden Plate Bags for Mother and Daughter

The Dresden Plate is very vivid in the smaller bag. I embellished Mother's bag with a little something more.

Instructions on page 66.

DRESDEN PLATE

PARTY BAG

Pineapple and Log Cabin Evening Bags

You will never regret having this one-of-a-kind evening bag. Take it to a party or use it when you are in a dressy mood.

Instructions on page 67.

Dresden Plate Bags for Mother and Daughter·········P. 64

(Materials)
Background fabric, batting······70cm × 40cm (27^1/$_2$″ × 15^3/$_4$″) each
Assorted scraps of print fabric
Backing fabric, lining fabric······70cm × 25cm (27^1/$_2$″ × 9^7/$_8$″) each

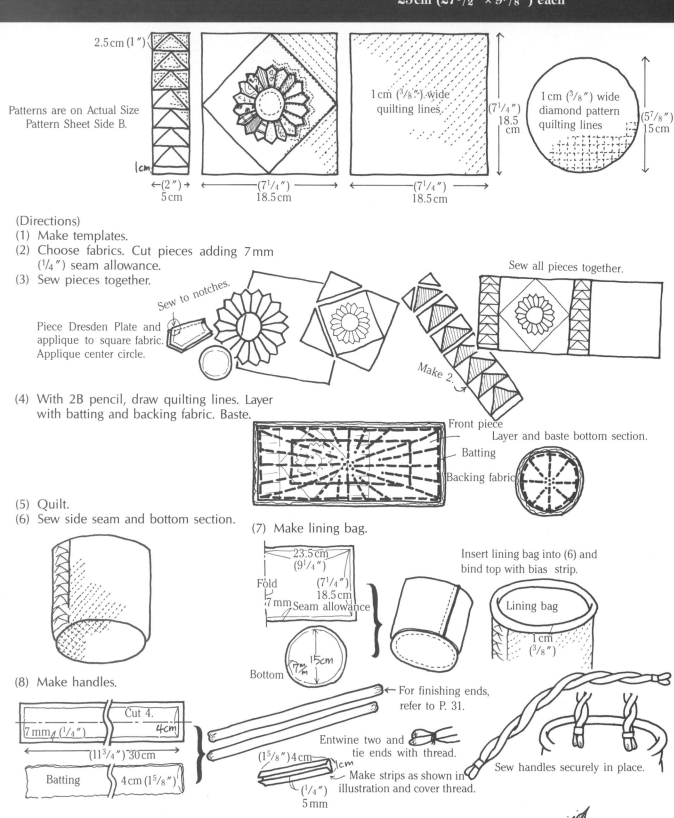

2.5cm (1″)

Patterns are on Actual Size Pattern Sheet Side B.

1cm

←(2″)→ 5cm

←(7^1/$_4$″)→ 18.5cm

1cm (3/8″) wide quilting lines

(7^1/$_4$″) 18.5cm

←(7^1/$_4$″)→ 18.5cm

1cm (3/8″) wide diamond pattern quilting lines

(5^7/$_8$″) 15cm

(Directions)
(1) Make templates.
(2) Choose fabrics. Cut pieces adding 7mm (1/4″) seam allowance.
(3) Sew pieces together.

Sew to notches.

Piece Dresden Plate and applique to square fabric. Applique center circle.

Sew all pieces together.

Make 2.

(4) With 2B pencil, draw quilting lines. Layer with batting and backing fabric. Baste.

Front piece

Batting

Backing fabric

Layer and baste bottom section.

(5) Quilt.
(6) Sew side seam and bottom section.

(7) Make lining bag.

23.5cm (9^1/$_4$″)

Fold

(7^1/$_4$″) 18.5cm

7mm Seam allowance

Bottom

7$_m$$_m$ 15cm

Insert lining bag into (6) and bind top with bias strip.

Lining bag

1cm (3/8″)

(8) Make handles.

Cut 4.

7mm (1/4″)

4cm

(11^3/$_4$″) 30cm

Batting 4cm (1^5/$_8$″)

For finishing ends, refer to P. 31.

Entwine two and tie ends with thread.

(1^5/$_8$″) 4cm

1cm

(1/4″) 5mm

Make strips as shown in illustration and cover thread.

Sew handles securely in place.

(Materials)
Satin······70cm × 30cm (27$\frac{1}{2}$″ × 11$\frac{3}{4}$″)
Assorted scraps of print fabric
Ribbon (3.5cm (1$\frac{3}{8}$″) wide)······250cm
(98$\frac{1}{2}$″)
Backing fabric, batting······70cm × 40cm
(27$\frac{1}{2}$″ × 15$\frac{3}{4}$″) each *

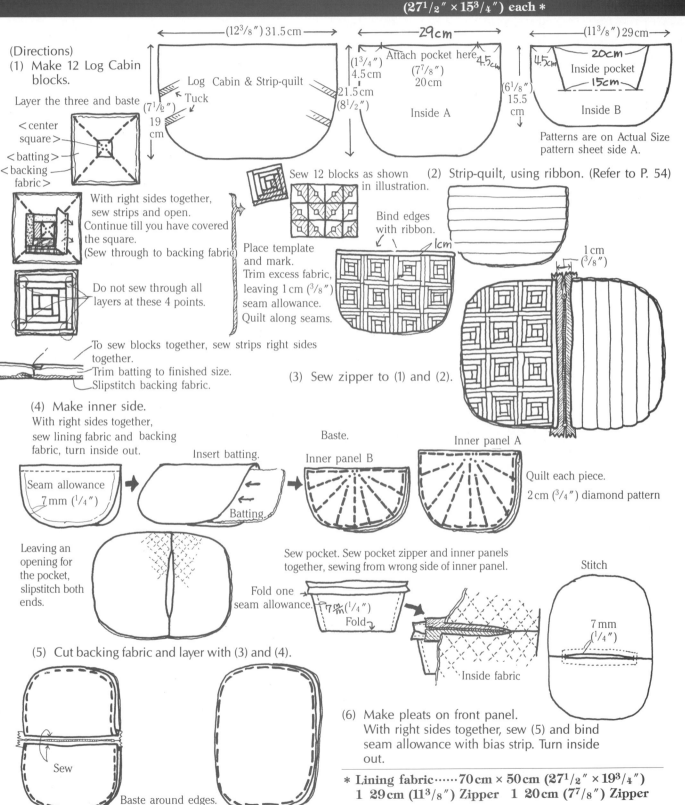

(Directions)
(1) Make 12 Log Cabin blocks.

Layer the three and baste

< center square >
< batting >
< backing fabric >

With right sides together, sew strips and open. Continue till you have covered the square. (Sew through to backing fabric)

Do not sew through all layers at these 4 points.

To sew blocks together, sew strips right sides together.
Trim batting to finished size.
Slipstitch backing fabric.

(12$\frac{3}{8}$″) 31.5cm

Log Cabin & Strip-quilt
Tuck
(7$\frac{1}{2}$″) 19 cm
21.5cm (8$\frac{1}{2}$″)

29cm

(1$\frac{3}{4}$″) 4.5cm
Attach pocket here 4.5cm
(7$\frac{7}{8}$″) 20cm
Inside A

(11$\frac{3}{8}$″) 29cm

4.5cm
20cm
Inside pocket
15cm
(6$\frac{1}{8}$″) 15.5 cm
Inside B

Patterns are on Actual Size pattern sheet side A.

Sew 12 blocks as shown in illustration.

Place template and mark.
Trim excess fabric, leaving 1 cm ($\frac{3}{8}$″) seam allowance.
Quilt along seams.

Bind edges with ribbon.

1cm

(2) Strip-quilt, using ribbon. (Refer to P. 54)

1 cm ($\frac{3}{8}$″)

(3) Sew zipper to (1) and (2).

(4) Make inner side.
With right sides together, sew lining fabric and backing fabric, turn inside out.

Seam allowance 7mm ($\frac{1}{4}$″)

Insert batting.
Batting
Baste.

Inner panel B
Inner panel A

Quilt each piece.
2cm ($\frac{3}{4}$″) diamond pattern

Leaving an opening for the pocket, slipstitch both ends.

Sew pocket. Sew pocket zipper and inner panels together, sewing from wrong side of inner panel.

Fold one seam allowance. 7mm ($\frac{1}{4}$″)
Fold

Inside fabric

Stitch

7 mm ($\frac{1}{4}$″)

(5) Cut backing fabric and layer with (3) and (4).

Sew

Baste around edges.

(6) Make pleats on front panel.
With right sides together, sew (5) and bind seam allowance with bias strip. Turn inside out.

* Lining fabric······70cm × 50cm (27$\frac{1}{2}$″ × 19$\frac{3}{4}$″)
1 29cm (11$\frac{3}{8}$″) Zipper 1 20cm (7$\frac{7}{8}$″) Zipper

Thousand Pyramid Tote Bags

A simple triangle pattern enhances these bags. I played with interesting fabrics for one of the handles and pieced the other handle.

Instructions on page 70.

Diamond Travel Bag
and Pouch

White quilting and a diamond border are in an asymmetrical placement in this soft and easy-to-use travel bag. The navy blue binding is the accent. The drawstring pouch is made by piecing the diamonds in a tube shape.

Instructions on page 71.

69

Thousand Pyramid Tote Bags
.... **P. 68**

(Materials)
Background fabric······60 cm × 30 cm
($23^1/_2$″ × $11^3/_4$″)
Assorted scraps of print fabric
Backing fabric······60 cm × 40 cm ($23^1/_2$″ × $15^3/_4$″)
Batting······60 cm × 50 cm ($23^1/_2$″ × $19^3/_4$″)

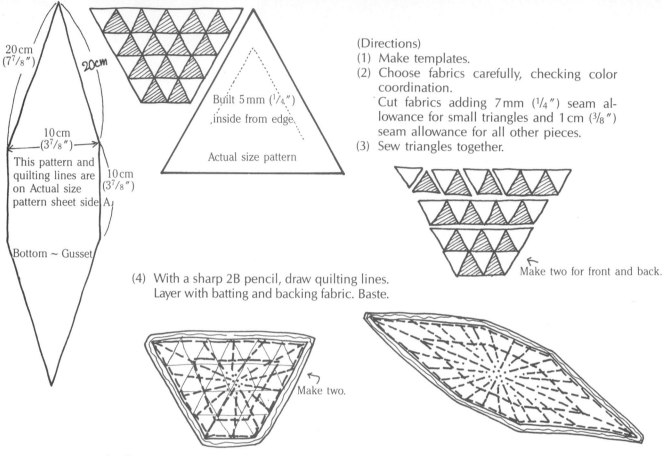

20 cm ($7^7/_8$″)

20cm

10 cm ($3^7/_8$″)

This pattern and quilting lines are on Actual size pattern sheet side A.

10 cm ($3^7/_8$″)

Bottom ~ Gusset

Built 5 mm ($^1/_4$″) inside from edge.

Actual size pattern

(Directions)
(1) Make templates.
(2) Choose fabrics carefully, checking color coordination.
Cut fabrics adding 7 mm ($^1/_4$″) seam allowance for small triangles and 1 cm ($^3/_8$″) seam allowance for all other pieces.
(3) Sew triangles together.

Make two for front and back.

(4) With a sharp 2B pencil, draw quilting lines. Layer with batting and backing fabric. Baste.

Make two.

(5) Quilt all sections.
Apply pattern to quilted sections and mark finished lines. Trim seam allowances to same width.

(6) Sew 3 sections in (5) together.
Bind seam allowance with bias strip.

(7) Sew bias strip on top edges of bag.
Attach polyester stuffing to bias strip and slip stitch.

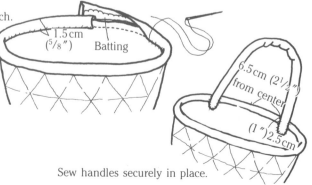

1.5 cm ($^5/_8$″)   Batting

6.5 cm ($2^1/_2$″) from center

(1″) 2.5 cm

(8) Attach handles.
With right sides together, fold fabric lengthwise in half and sew. Turn inside out. Insert polyester stuffing.

Sew handles securely in place.

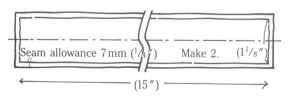

Seam allowance 7 mm ($^1/_4$″)   Make 2.   ($1^1/_8$″)

←———————— (15″) ————————→

Diamond Travel Bag and Pouch......P. 69

(Materials)
Background fabric······125cm × 50cm
(49¹/₄″ × 19³/₄″)
Assorted scraps of print fabric
Backing fabric, batting······125cm × 70cm
(49¹/₄″ × 27¹/₂″)
2 60cm (23¹/₂″) zipper

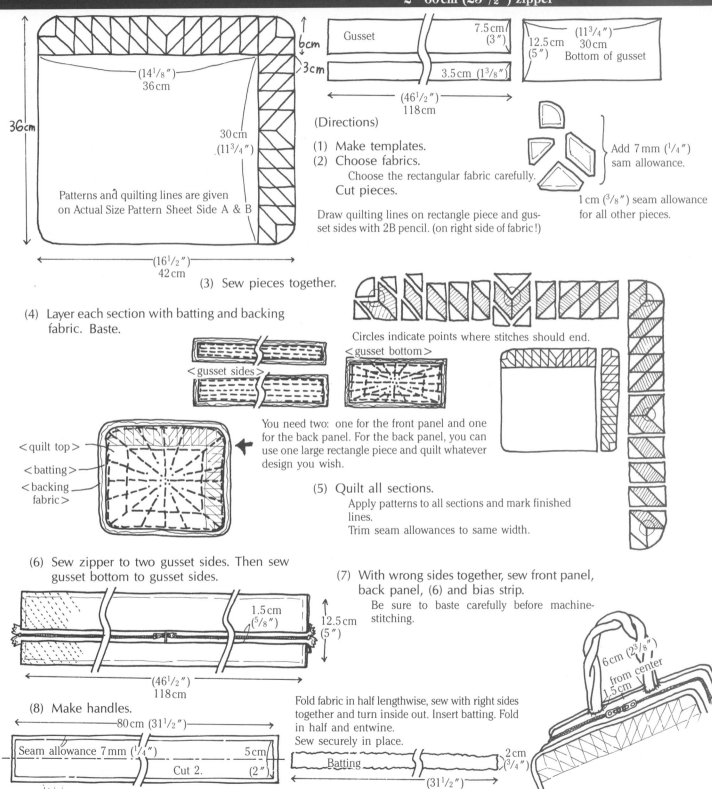

36cm

(14¹/₈″)
36cm

6cm

3cm

30cm
(11³/₄″)

Patterns and quilting lines are given
on Actual Size Pattern Sheet Side A & B

(16¹/₂″)
42cm

Gusset   7.5cm
                                                    (3″)

3.5cm (1³/₈″)

(46¹/₂″)
118cm

(11³/₄″)
12.5cm   30cm
(5″)   Bottom of gusset

Add 7mm (¹/₄″)
sam allowance.

1cm (³/₈″) seam allowance
for all other pieces.

(Directions)

(1) Make templates.
(2) Choose fabrics.
    Choose the rectangular fabric carefully.
Cut pieces.

Draw quilting lines on rectangle piece and gusset sides with 2B pencil. (on right side of fabric!)

(3) Sew pieces together.

(4) Layer each section with batting and backing
    fabric. Baste.

Circles indicate points where stitches should end.

<gusset sides>

<gusset bottom>

You need two: one for the front panel and one
for the back panel. For the back panel, you can
use one large rectangle piece and quilt whatever
design you wish.

<quilt top>
<batting>
<backing
fabric>

(5) Quilt all sections.
    Apply patterns to all sections and mark finished
    lines.
    Trim seam allowances to same width.

(6) Sew zipper to two gusset sides. Then sew
    gusset bottom to gusset sides.

(7) With wrong sides together, sew front panel,
    back panel, (6) and bias strip.
        Be sure to baste carefully before machine-
    stitching.

1.5cm
(⁵/₈″)

12.5cm
(5″)

(46¹/₂″)
118cm

6cm (2³/₈″)
from center
1.5cm

(8) Make handles.

80cm (31¹/₂″)

Seam allowance 7mm (¹/₄″)   5cm
                    Cut 2.   (2″)

Fold fabric in half lengthwise, sew with right sides
together and turn inside out. Insert batting. Fold
in half and entwine.
Sew securely in place.

Batting

2cm
(³/₄″)

(31¹/₂″)
80cm

71

Simple Four-patch
Tote Bags

I have used a basic patchwork pattern for this handy tote bag. The corners are turned in and rounded off. Happy shopping!

Instructions on pages 74, 75.

MS. CHUCK'S
PATCHWORK
[pách'wûrk']

A kind of fancy work in which pieces of cloth differing in color and shape are sewn together,

oftentimes to form a design,

and which is used in covering quilts,

pillows, etc.; hence,

a similarly variegated or checkered appearance or scene,

as a patchwork of fields

(Materials)
Background fabric······70cm × 70cm
(27$\frac{1}{2}$″ × 27$\frac{1}{2}$″) square
Assorted scraps of print fabric
Backing fabric, batting······70cm × 40cm
(27$\frac{1}{2}$″ × 15$\frac{3}{4}$″) each

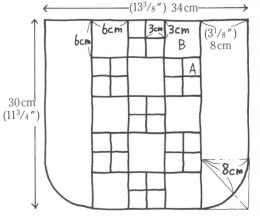

(13$\frac{3}{8}$″) 34cm

6cm 6cm 3cm 3cm (3$\frac{1}{8}$″) 8cm

B

A

30cm (11$\frac{3}{4}$″)

8cm

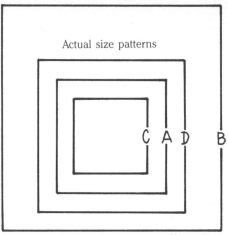

Actual size patterns

C A D B

Directions are the same for small size bag.

❤ Bag (small) ❤

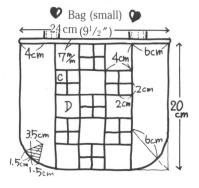

24cm (9$\frac{1}{2}$″)

4cm 7$\frac{m}{m}$ 4cm 6cm

C

2cm

D 2cm

20cm

3.5cm

1.5cm 1.5cm

6cm

(Directions)
(1) Make cardboard templates.
(2) Choose fabrics.
   Cut pieces adding 7mm (¼″) seam allowance.
   Arrange all pieces in order and check color coordination.

(3) Sew pieces together.

(4) Layer (3) with batting and backing fabric. Baste. Layer back panel with batting and backing fabric.

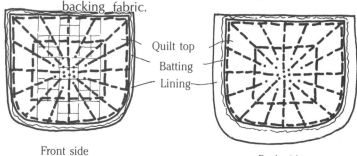

Quilt top
Batting
Lining

Front side

Back side

You will need piping: 60cm (23$\frac{1}{2}$″) long × 1
40cm (15$\frac{3}{4}$″) long × 4······for handles

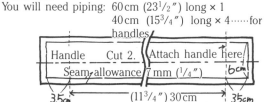

Handle   Cut 2.   Attach handle here.
Seam allowance 7mm (¼″)   6cm
3.5cm   (11$\frac{3}{4}$″) 30cm   3.5cm

Apply piping to both edges of handles.

❤ Bag (Middle) ❤

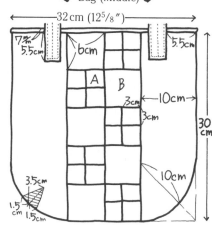

32cm (12$\frac{5}{8}$″)

7$\frac{m}{m}$ 5.5cm   6cm   5.5cm

A B

3cm 10cm
3cm

30cm

3.5cm   10cm

1.5cm 1.5cm

Piping: 85cm (33$\frac{1}{2}$″) long × 1

Cut backing fabric for back panel larger. It will be used to bind seam allowance.

Handle   Cut 2.
Seam allowance 7mm (¼″)   6cm
(21$\frac{5}{8}$″) 55cm

Handles are sewn on outside of bag.

(5) Quilt.

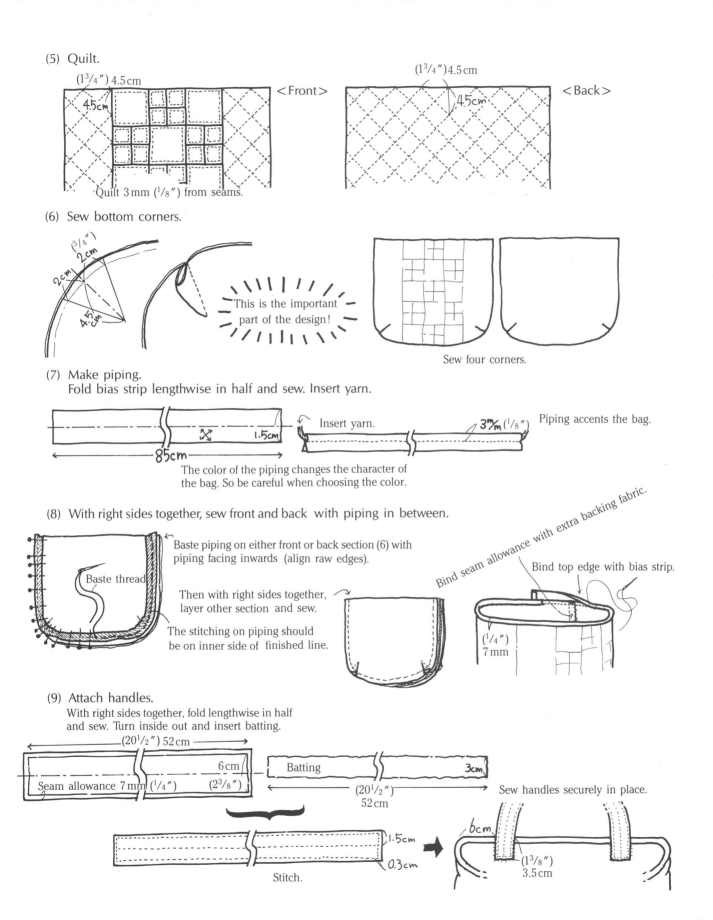

(1¾") 4.5 cm

4.5cm

＜Front＞

(1¾")4.5cm

4.5cm

＜Back＞

Quilt 3 mm (⅛") from seams.

(6) Sew bottom corners.

(³⁄₄")
2cm

2cm

4.5cm

This is the important
part of the design!

Sew four corners.

(7) Make piping.
Fold bias strip lengthwise in half and sew. Insert yarn.

1.5cm

85cm

Insert yarn.

3㎜(⅛")

Piping accents the bag.

The color of the piping changes the character of
the bag. So be careful when choosing the color.

(8) With right sides together, sew front and back with piping in between.

Baste thread

Baste piping on either front or back section (6) with
piping facing inwards (align raw edges).

Then with right sides together,
layer other section and sew.

The stitching on piping should
be on inner side of finished line.

Bind seam allowance with extra backing fabric.

Bind top edge with bias strip.

(¼")
7 mm

(9) Attach handles.
With right sides together, fold lengthwise in half
and sew. Turn inside out and insert batting.

(20½") 52 cm

6cm

Seam allowance 7 mm (¼")   (2³⁄₈")

Batting

3cm

(20½")
52 cm

Sew handles securely in place.

1.5cm

0.3cm

Stitch.

6cm

(1³⁄₈")
3.5 cm

Sunflower Drawstring Purse

This is a very quick and easy pattern. When the center part seems too dominant, choose the fabric for the surrounding pieces carefully or even change the size of the oval. You could even use a printed pattern fabric.

Instructions on pages 78, 79.

PATCHWORK

[pách'wûrk']

A kind of fancy work in which pieces of cloth differing in color and shape are sewn together,

oftentimes to form a design,

and which is used in covering quilts,

pillows, etc.; hence,

a similar variegated or checkered appearance or scene,

as a patchwork of fields

Sunflower Drawstring Purse ·······PP. 76, 77

(Materials)
Assorted scraps of print fabric
Background fabric (satin)······40 cm × 25 cm
(15³/₄″ × 9⁷/₈″)
Fabric for drawstring opening······40 cm ×
30 cm (15³/₄″ × 11³/₄″)
Lining fabric, backing fabric, batting······
60 cm × 30 cm (23¹/₂″ × 11³/₄″) each
Cord······160 cm (63″)

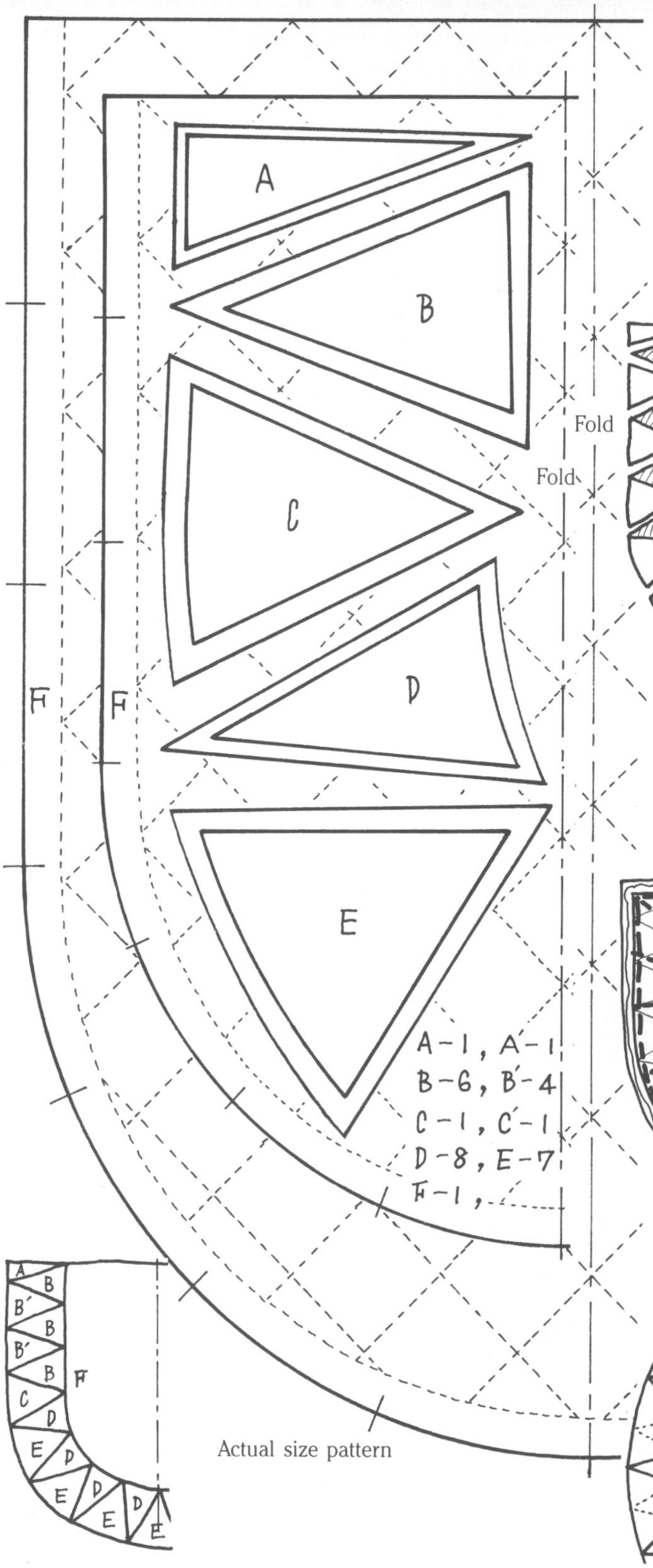

(Directions)
(1) Make cardboard templates.
(2) Cut pieces adding 7 mm (¹/₄″) seam allowance.
   Arrange pieces in order and check color coordination.

(3) Sew pieces together.

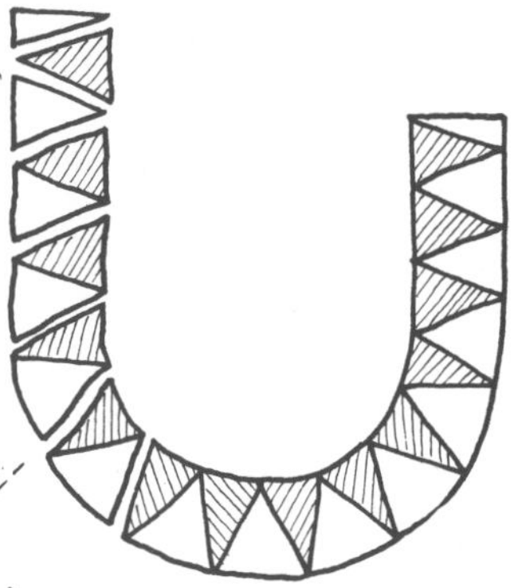

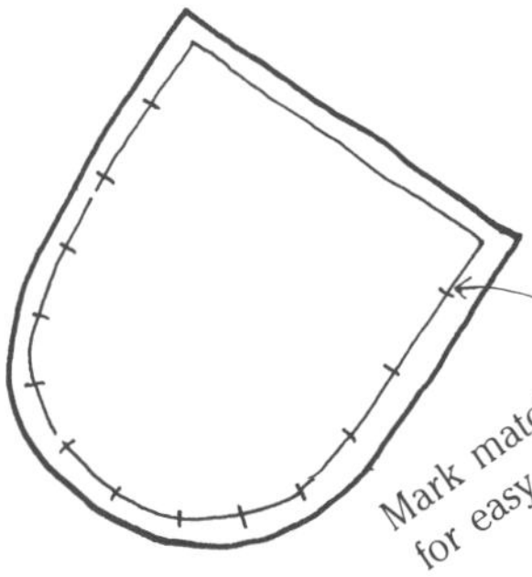

Mark matching dots for easy sewing.

(4) With a sharp 2B pencil, draw quilting lines. Layer with batting and backing fabric. Baste.

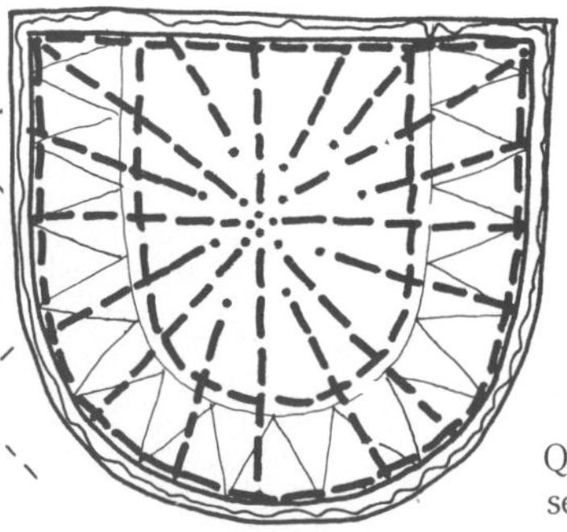

Make two: one for the front and one for the back.

(5) Quilt.

Quilting lines for pieced triangle section is shown in illustration.

A
B
C
D
E

Fold
Fold

F   F

A – 1, A – 1
B – 6, B – 4
C – 1, C – 1
D – 8, E – 7
F – 1,

Actual size pattern

Don't forget to quilt in the ditch as shown. It makes a big difference!

(6) Make piping.
   Large bag: 50 cm (19$\frac{3}{4}$″)
   Small bag: 41 cm (16$\frac{1}{8}$″)

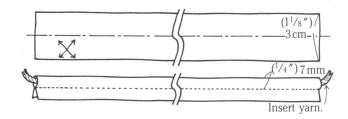

(7) With right sides together, sew (5) with piping in between.

(8) Sew drawstring opening section.

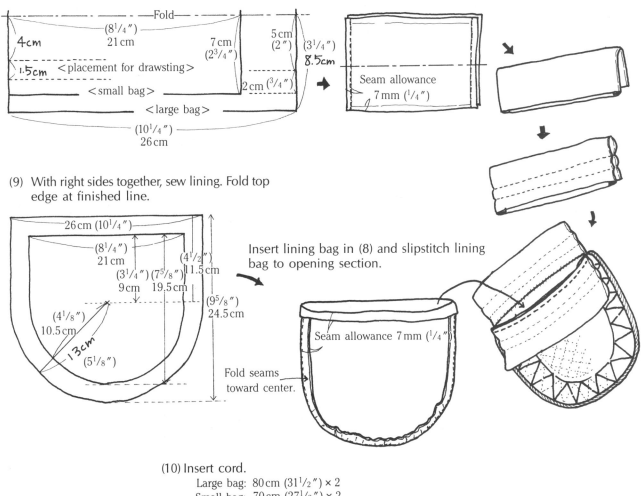

Fold

(8$\frac{1}{4}$″)
21 cm

4 cm

1.5 cm   <placement for drawsting>

<small bag>

<large bag>

(10$\frac{1}{4}$″)
26 cm

7 cm
(2$\frac{3}{4}$″)

2 cm ($\frac{3}{4}$″)

5 cm
(2″)

(3$\frac{1}{4}$″)
8.5 cm

Seam allowance
7 mm (¼″)

(9) With right sides together, sew lining. Fold top edge at finished line.

26 cm (10$\frac{1}{4}$″)

(8$\frac{1}{4}$″)
21 cm

(3$\frac{1}{4}$″)(7$\frac{5}{8}$″)
9 cm   19.5 cm

(4$\frac{1}{8}$″)
10.5 cm

13 cm
(5$\frac{1}{8}$″)

(4$\frac{1}{2}$″)
11.5 cm

(9$\frac{5}{8}$″)
24.5 cm

Insert lining bag in (8) and slipstitch lining bag to opening section.

Seam allowance 7 mm (¼″)

Fold seams toward center.

(10) Insert cord.
   Large bag: 80 cm (31$\frac{1}{2}$″) × 2
   Small bag: 70 cm (27$\frac{1}{2}$″) × 2

Try attaching metal ornaments to cord ends.

MS.CHUCK'S
PATCHWORK
[pách'wûrk']

A kind of fancy work in which pieces of cloth differing in color and shape are sewn together

oftentimes to form a design,

and which is used in covering quilts,

pillows, etc.; hence,

a similarly variegated or checkered appearance or scene,

as a patchwork of fields.

TWOWAY BAG

Two-way Bags

This is one of the more challenging bags but it is worth the try. It is round and cute to carry around. The small handle accents the bag.

Instructions on pages 82, 83.

Two-way Bags··················PP. 80, 81

(Materials)
Background fabric······45 cm × 30 cm
($17^3/_4"$ × $11^3/_4"$)
Backing fabric, batting······45 cm × 40 cm
($17^3/_4"$ × $15^3/_4"$) each
Assorted scraps of print fabric
2 Hooks 1 36 cm ($14^1/_4"$) Zipper
1 13 cm ($5^1/_8"$) Zipper

Actual Size Pattern

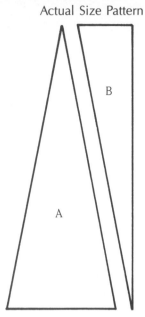

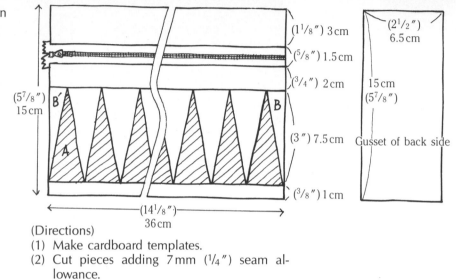

(5⁷/₈″) 15 cm

(1¹/₈″) 3 cm
(⁵/₈″) 1.5 cm
(³/₄″) 2 cm
(3″) 7.5 cm
(³/₈″) 1 cm

(2¹/₂″) 6.5 cm
15 cm (5⁷/₈″)
Gusset of back side

←————— (14¹/₈″) —————→
36 cm

(Directions)
(1) Make cardboard templates.
(2) Cut pieces adding 7 mm (¼″) seam allowance.
     Arrange pieces in order and check color coordination.
     Change pieces that look out of place.

(3) Sew pieces together.
     Start piecing triangles and then sew on strips.

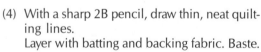

(4) With a sharp 2B pencil, draw thin, neat quilting lines.
     Layer with batting and backing fabric. Baste.

(5) With right sides together, sew background fabric and backing fabric of lid section with zipper in between. Insert batting between two layers. Baste.

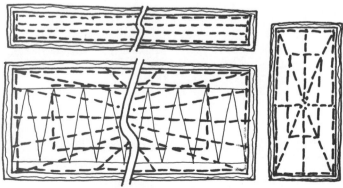

(6) Quilt. (refer to P. 6)

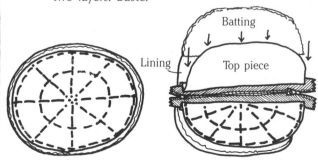

Batting
Lining
Top piece

(7) Make piping.

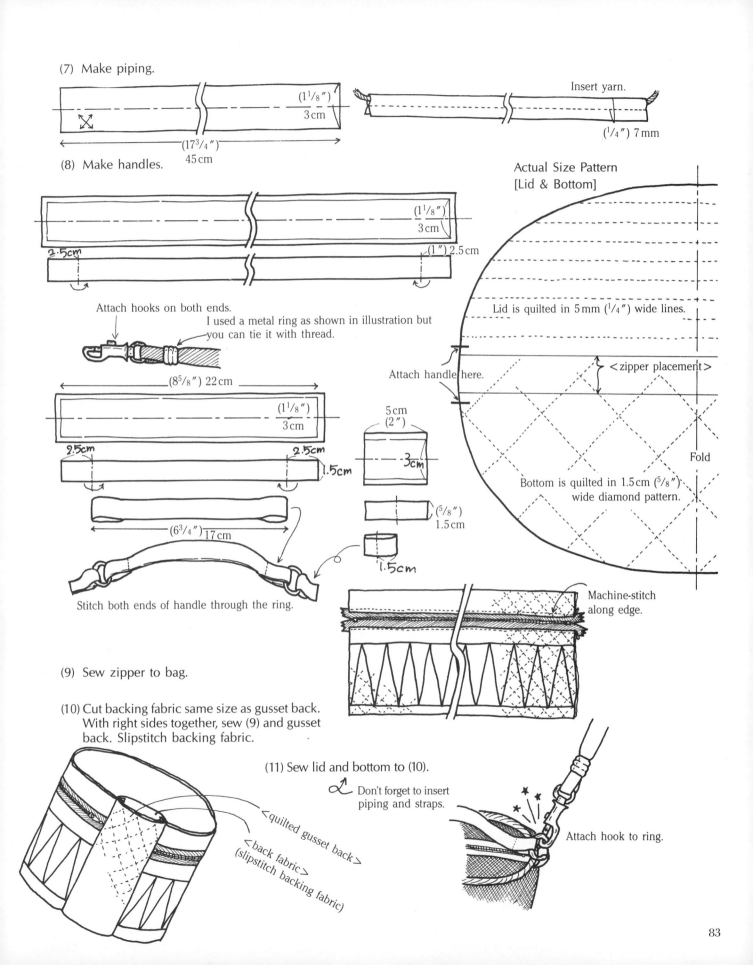

Insert yarn.

($1^1/_8''$)
3 cm

($1/_4''$) 7 mm

($17^3/_4''$)
45 cm

(8) Make handles.

($1^1/_8''$)
3 cm

2.5 cm

(1") 2.5 cm

Attach hooks on both ends.

I used a metal ring as shown in illustration but you can tie it with thread.

($8^5/_8''$) 22 cm

($1^1/_8''$)
3 cm

2.5 cm

2.5 cm

1.5 cm

($6^3/_4''$) 17 cm

Stitch both ends of handle through the ring.

5 cm
(2")

3 cm

($5/_8''$)
1.5 cm

1.5 cm

Actual Size Pattern
[Lid & Bottom]

Lid is quilted in 5 mm ($1/_4''$) wide lines.

< zipper placement >

Attach handle here.

Fold

Bottom is quilted in 1.5 cm ($5/_8''$) wide diamond pattern.

Machine-stitch along edge.

(9) Sew zipper to bag.

(10) Cut backing fabric same size as gusset back. With right sides together, sew (9) and gusset back. Slipstitch backing fabric.

(11) Sew lid and bottom to (10).

α↗ Don't forget to insert piping and straps.

<quilted gusset back>

<back fabric>
(slipstitch backing fabric)

Attach hook to ring.

Yo Yo Quilt Opera Bag

The blue yo yo bag is made from lace fabric and embellished with embroidery. The purple bag is made from Japanese material. Try experimenting with different embroidery stitches and have fun!

Instructions on pages 86, 87.

Yo Yo Quilt Opera Bags

...... **PP. 84, 85**

(Materials)
Background fabric (bag), lining fabric······
60 cm × 30 cm (23$\frac{1}{2}$″ × 11$\frac{3}{4}$″)
Assorted scraps of print fabric
Backing fabric, batting······60 cm × 15 cm
(23$\frac{1}{2}$″ × 6″) each
 # 25 Embroidery floss
2 Cords······1 m (39$\frac{3}{8}$″) each

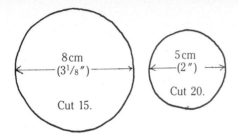

8 cm
(3$\frac{1}{8}$″)
Cut 15.

5 cm
(2″)
Cut 20.

(Directions)
(1) Make yo yos.
    (a) Cut fabric adding 5 mm ($\frac{1}{4}$″) seam allowance.
        Large circle: make about 15
        Small circle: make about 20
        This is only an approximate number and it may differ according to the placement of the yo yos.
    (b) Fold seam allowance and sew 1–2 mm ($\frac{1}{16}$″ – $\frac{1}{8}$″) from edge.

[Running Stitch]

···· 4 3 2 1
out-in-out-in

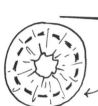

Stitch two lines on yo yo for a neat finish.

[French Knots Stitch]

Wrap floss twice.

1 out   3 in

[Spider Web Stitch]

out 2 in
14 13 4 in 3 out
in
15 out
7
out 8 in 9 out 10 in
6 5 in 11 out
in out 1 out

Go under 2 lines, go back wrapping one line and so on. Do not stitch fabric.

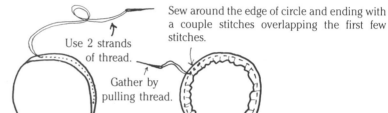

Sew around the edge of circle and ending with a couple stitches overlapping the first few stitches.

Use 2 strands of thread.

Gather by pulling thread.

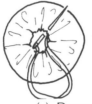

    (c) Decorate with embroidery. You may use other embroidery stitches not shown here.

(2) Arrange yo yos on paper cut the size of bag (12 cm × 38 cm (4$\frac{3}{4}$″ × 15″)). After you have decided on the placement of yo yos, connect them using buttonhole stitch.

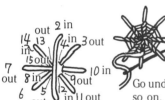

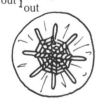

[Buttonhole stitch]

out
4
2 1 in
out   3 in

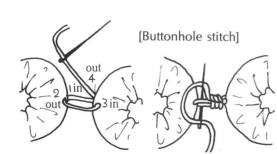

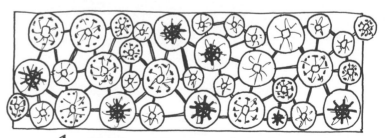

There is no right and wrong in the placement of the yo yos. Experiment with different arrangements.

[Feather-stitch]

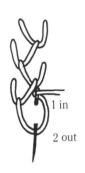

1 in

2 out

(3) Make bag.

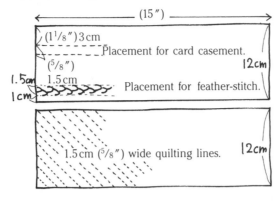

← (15″) →

(1⅛″) 3 cm

Placement for card casement.

(⅝″)

12 cm

1.5 cm

1.5 cm

Placement for feather-stitch.

1 cm

1.5 cm (⅝″) wide quilting lines.

1.5 cm (⅝″) wide quilting lines.

12 cm

Bottom

(4¾″)

12 cm

(a) Layer all pieces with batting and backing fabric.
Baste.
(b) Quilt.
(c) Sew fabric to bag.
(d) Sew side seams. Sew bottom section.

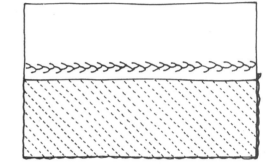

(e) Make lining bag.

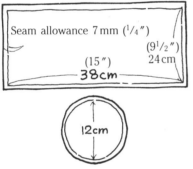

Seam allowance 7 mm (¼″)

(9½″)

24 cm

(15″)

38 cm

12 cm

(f) Insert (e) into (d). Bind top edges with bias strip.

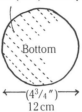

With right sides together, sew one edge to bag. Fold other edge to seam line and slipstitch. (Slipstitch to lining)

(g) Sew two strips for cord casement.

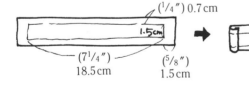

(¼″) 0.7 cm

1.5 cm

(7¼″)

18.5 cm

(⅝″)

1.5 cm

1 cm

(⅜″)

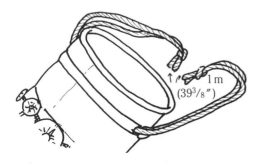

1 m

(39⅜″)

(4) Whipstitch (2) to (3). Be sure to sew side seams of yo yo.
(5) Insert cord.

MS.CHU's
PATCHWORK
[pách'wûrk']

A kind of fancy work in which pieces of cloth differing in color and shape are sewn together,

oftentimes to form a design,

and which is used in covering quilts,

pillows, etc.; hence,

a similarly variegated or checkered appearance or scene,

as a patchwork of fields.

Sampler Clutch Bags

Make those patterns that you have always wanted to make and piece them with a border in between. I have inserted piping to accent the different patterns and to give it a sturdy finish. The bag is handy to take to the office, or add another row and make it into a pillow. You will enjoy it.

Instructions on pages 90, 91.

CLUTCH BAG

Sampler Clutch Bags

.... PP. 88, 89

(Materials)
Background fabric······80cm × 40cm
(31¹/₂″ × 15³/₄″)
Assorted scraps of print fabric
Backing fabric, batting······70cm × 40cm
(27¹/₂″ × 15³/₄″) each
1 35cm (13³/₄″) Zipper
Cardboard······40cm × 10cm (15³/₄″ × 4″)

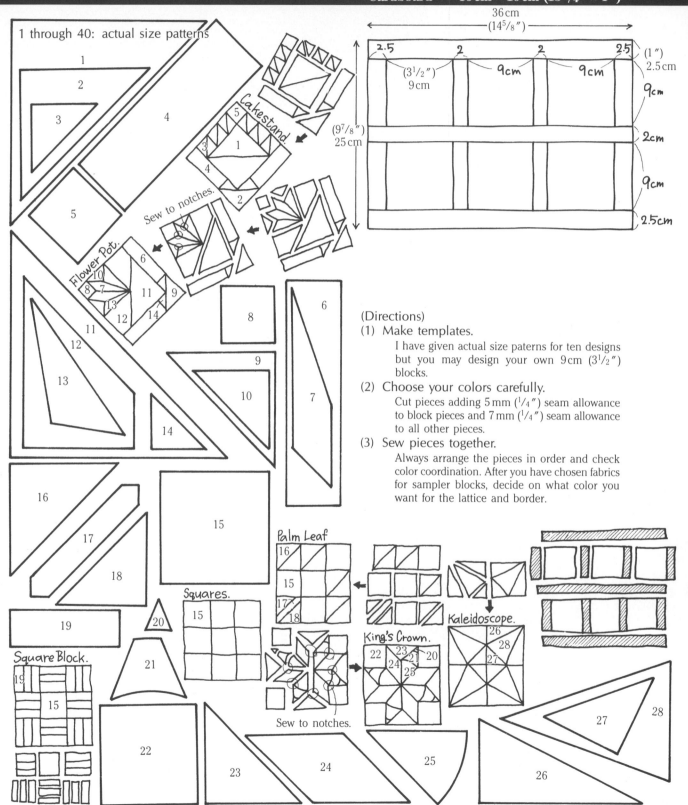

1 through 40: actual size patterns

36cm
(14⁵/₈″)

2.5   2   2   2.5   (1″) 2.5cm

(3¹/₂″) 9cm   9cm   9cm   9cm

(9⁷/₈″) 25cm   2cm

9cm

2.5cm

Cakestand.

Sew to notches.

Flower Pot.

Palm Leaf

Squares.

Square Block.

King's Crown.

Kaleidoscope.

(Directions)
(1) Make templates.
    I have given actual size paterns for ten designs but you may design your own 9cm (3¹/₂″) blocks.
(2) Choose your colors carefully.
    Cut pieces adding 5mm (¹/₄″) seam allowance to block pieces and 7mm (¹/₄″) seam allowance to all other pieces.
(3) Sew pieces together.
    Always arrange the pieces in order and check color coordination. After you have chosen fabrics for sampler blocks, decide on what color you want for the lattice and border.

Sew to notches.

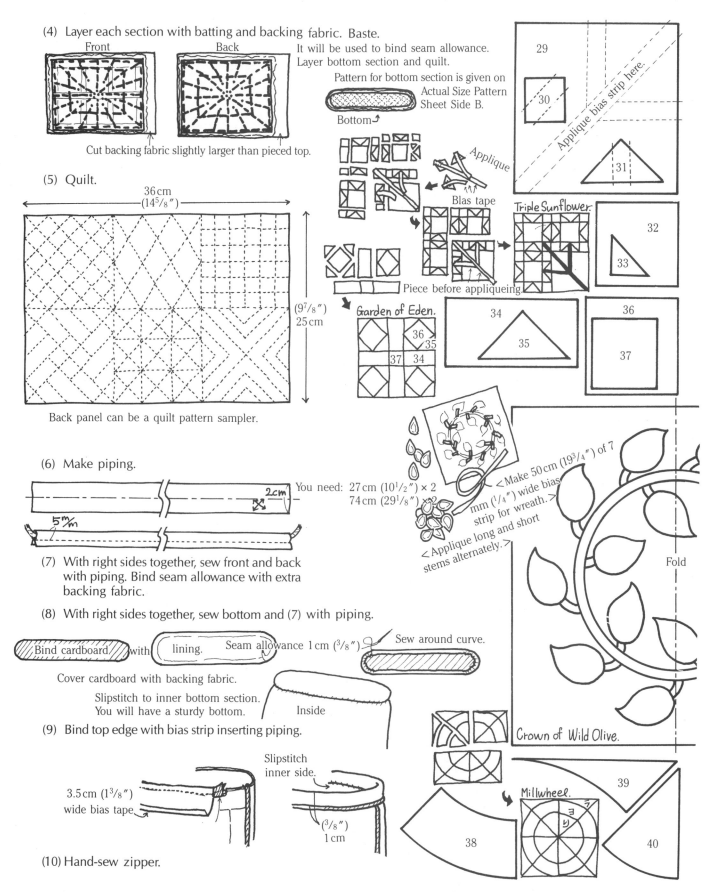

(4) Layer each section with batting and backing fabric. Baste.

Front

Back

Cut backing fabric slightly larger than pieced top.

It will be used to bind seam allowance.
Layer bottom section and quilt.

Pattern for bottom section is given on Actual Size Pattern Sheet Side B.

Bottom↲

(5) Quilt.

36cm
(14⁵⁄₈″)

(9⁷⁄₈″)
25cm

Back panel can be a quilt pattern sampler.

Applique

Bias tape

Triple Sunflower.

Piece before appliqueing.

Garden of Eden.

	36	
	35	
37	34	

29

30

31

32

33

34

35

36

37

(6) Make piping.

2cm

5 m/m

You need: 27cm (10¹⁄₂″) × 2
74cm (29¹⁄₈″) ×2

(7) With right sides together, sew front and back with piping. Bind seam allowance with extra backing fabric.

(8) With right sides together, sew bottom and (7) with piping.

Bind cardboard with lining.

Seam allowance 1cm (³⁄₈″)

Sew around curve.

Cover cardboard with backing fabric.

Slipstitch to inner bottom section.
You will have a sturdy bottom.

Inside

(9) Bind top edge with bias strip inserting piping.

Slipstitch
inner side.

3.5cm (1³⁄₈″)
wide bias tape

(³⁄₈″)
1cm

(10) Hand-sew zipper.

< Make 50cm (19³⁄₄″) of 7 mm (¹⁄₄″) wide bias strip for wreath. >

< Applique long and short stems alternately. >

Applique bias strip here.

Fold

Crown of Wild Olive.

Millwheel.

38

39

40

Appliqued Flower

A present from Mother to Son! He will certainly be very proud and take good care of it. Appliqued quilts involve much quilting. I have closely quilted the bag so it can be washed in the washing machine, as you are aware that children just love to come home with dirty clothes.

Instructions on pages 94, 95.

Basket Bag for Mother and A Doggy for Me

APPLIQUÉ BAG

Appliqued Flower Basket Bag .... P. 92

(Materials)
Background fabric······130 cm × 70 cm
(51¼″ × 27½″)
Assorted scraps of print fabric
Backing fabric, batting······120 cm × 60 cm
(47¼″ × 23½″)
Belting······60 cm × 10 cm (23½″ × 4″)

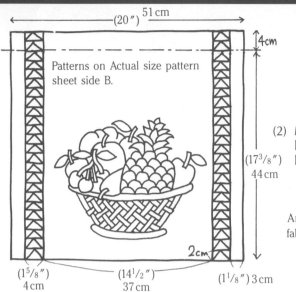

Patterns on Actual size pattern sheet side B.

(20″) 51 cm
4 cm
(17³/₈″) 44 cm
(1⁵/₈″) 4 cm
(14½″) 37 cm
2 cm
(1¹/₈″) 3 cm

(Directions)

(1) Decide what color bag you want.
Place fabric on Actual Size Pattern Sheet and trace design on right side of fabric.

(If the color you choose is dark, try tracing against window.)

(2) Marking on the right side of fabric, cut applique pieces adding 5 mm (¼″) seam allowance.

Arrange pieces on background fabric and check color balance.

Draw with 2B pencil.

Seam allowance 1 cm (³/₈″)

(3) Applique all pieces, starting from bottom layer pieces.

(4) Sew triangles together. Then sew to appliqued top.

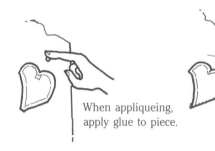

When appliqueing, apply glue to piece.

Turn seam allowance with needle tip and blind-stitch (clip where necessary).

Lift glue with needle tip after stitching.

(5) Draw quilting lines, layer with batting and backing fabric. Baste. Do the same for back.

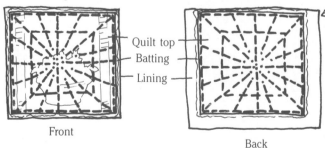

Quilt top
Batting
Lining

Front

Back

Cut backing fabric larger than background fabric. Use it to bind seam allowance.

(6) Quilt.

(7) With right sides together, sew front and back.

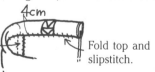

4 cm

Bind seam allowance with extra backing fabric.

Fold top and slipstitch.

(8) Make handles.

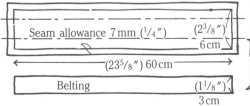

Seam allowance 7 mm (¼″)
(2³/₈″) 6 cm
(23⁵/₈″) 60 cm
Belting
(1¹/₈″)
3 cm

With right sides together, fold strip lengthwise in half and sew.
Turn inside out and insert batting.
Sew 1 cm (³/₈″) from edge.

(³/₈″) 1 cm

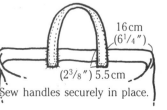

16 cm (6¼″)

(2³/₈″) 5.5 cm

Sew handles securely in place.

Appliqued Terrier Bag

P. 93

(Materials)
Background fabric, batting······60 cm ×
60 cm (23$^1/_2$″ × 23$^1/_2$″) each
Assorted scraps of print fabric
Backing fabric······70 cm × 60 cm (27$^1/_2$″ ×
23$^1/_2$″)
1 45 cm (17$^3/_4$″) Zipper

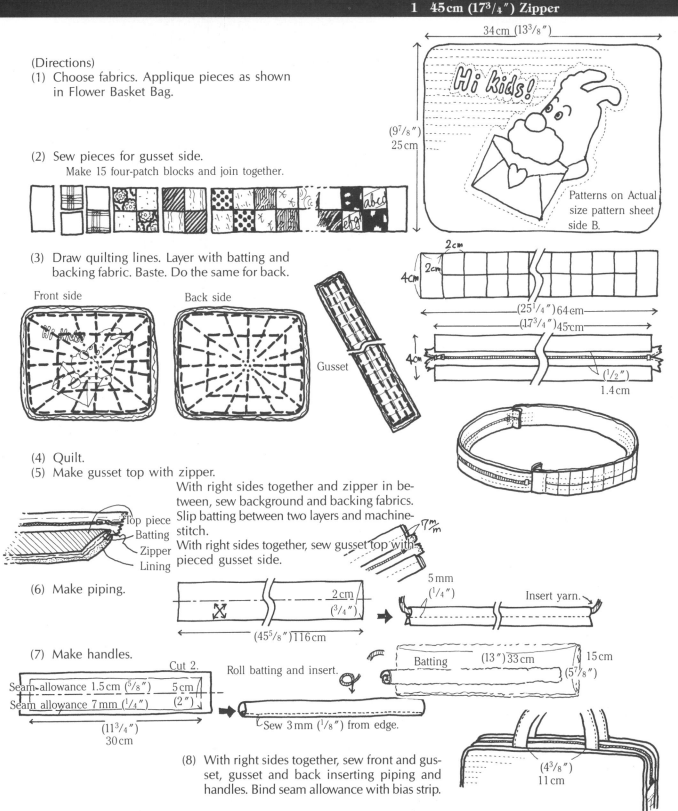

(Directions)
(1) Choose fabrics. Applique pieces as shown
in Flower Basket Bag.

(2) Sew pieces for gusset side.
Make 15 four-patch blocks and join together.

(3) Draw quilting lines. Layer with batting and
backing fabric. Baste. Do the same for back.

Front side

Back side

Gusset

Patterns on Actual
size pattern sheet
side B.

34 cm (13$^3/_8$″)

(9$^7/_8$″)
25 cm

2 cm

2 cm

4 cm

(25$^1/_4$″) 64 cm

(17$^3/_4$″) 45 cm

4 cm

(1/2″)
1.4 cm

(4) Quilt.
(5) Make gusset top with zipper.
With right sides together and zipper in between, sew background and backing fabrics.
Slip batting between two layers and machine-
stitch.
With right sides together, sew gusset top with
pieced gusset side.

Top piece
Batting
Zipper
Lining

7$^m/_m$

(6) Make piping.

5 mm
(1/4″)

Insert yarn.

2 cm
(3/4″)

(45$^5/_8$″) 116 cm

(7) Make handles.

Cut 2.

Seam allowance 1.5 cm (5/8″)   5 cm

Seam allowance 7 mm (1/4″)   (2″)

(11$^3/_4$″)
30 cm

Roll batting and insert.

Batting   (13″) 33 cm   15 cm
(5$^7/_8$″)

Sew 3 mm (1/8″) from edge.

(8) With right sides together, sew front and gusset, gusset and back inserting piping and
handles. Bind seam allowance with bias strip.

(4$^3/_8$″)
11 cm

I used sharply contrasting colors. The strips are sewn in sequences and it is easy to assemble this bag. Do you like it?

Instructions on page 3.

STRING

Strip-quilted Travel Case and Pouch